Strategy Driven for Success Handbook
Deploy Strategies – Achieve Objectives – Celebrate Successes

Strategy Driven for Success Handbook
Deploy Strategies – Achieve Objectives – Celebrate Successes

Rod Baxter

2015

Copyright © 2015 by Rod Baxter

All rights reserved. This book or any portion thereof may not be reproduced or used in any manner whatsoever without the express written permission of the publisher, except for the use of brief quotations in a book review or scholarly journal.

First Edition: 2015
Second Edition: 2016

ISBN 978-1-329-61937-1

Value Generation Partners, LLC
8083 San Vista Circle
Naples, Florida 34109
info@valuegenerationpartners.com

www.valuegenerationpartners.com

Contents

Introduction: Strategy Driven for Success 1
   Define Purpose, Vision, Mission, and Values 3
      Purpose Statement 3
      Vision Statement 3
      Mission Statement 3
      Core Values 4

Step One: Set the Strategic Goals 5
   Collect Voice of… as input to SWOT Analysis 6
      Voice of Customer 7
      Voice of Business 8
      Voice of Employee 9
      Voice of Process 10
      Voice of Competitor 11
   Create SIPOCs as Input to SWOT Analysis 12
   Conduct SWOT Analysis to Draft Strategic Goals 13
   Draft SMART Strategic Goals and Objectives 16
   Conduct Force Field on Drafted Strategic Goals 18
   Define, Communicate, and Cascade Strategy Maps 20

Step Two: Understand the KPIs 23

Step Three: Create Cultural Engagement 25
   Change Leadership 26
   Conflict Resolution 30
   Consensus Building 32
   Motivating Individuals 34
   Team Building 38

Step Four: Construct the Initiatives 45
   Identify Potential Initiatives and Projects 46
   Prioritize Potential Initiatives and Projects 47
   Align Prioritized Initiatives and Projects with Strategies .. 50

Step Five: Execute with Rigor and Discipline 53
   Project Management (PM) for Success 54
      PM Step One: Set-up the Project 57
      PM Step Two: Understand the Requirements 57
      PM Step Three: Create the Team 58
      PM Step Four: Construct the Plan 58
      PM Step Five: Execute the Plan 59

Contents

    PM Step Six: Sign-off and Close the Project 59
    PM Step Seven: Salute the Team 60
  Problem Solving (PS) for Success 60
    PS Step One: State Problem and Goal 62
    PS Step Two: Understand Current Condition 63
    PS Step Three: Conduct Root Cause Analysis 63
    PS Step Four: Construct Solutions 64
    PS Step Five: Execute Solutions 65
    PS Step Six: Sustain Solutions 66
    PS Step Seven: Salute the Team 67
  Workshop Facilitation (WF) for Success 67
    WF Step One: Set-up the Workshop Charter 69
    WF Step Two: Understand the Logistics 69
    WF Step Three: Create the Team 70
    WF Step Four: Clarify Roles and Responsibilities 70
    WF Step Five: Execute the Workshop 70
    WF Step Six: Share Status of Workshop 71
    WF Step Seven: Salute the Team 72

Step Six: Sustain Results with Scorecards 73
  Balanced and Cascading Scorecards 74

Step Seven: Salute the Organization 77

Summary: Strategy Driven for Success 79

Index 81

With the purchase of this book, you are eligible to receive a complementary MS Excel® file, which contains the templates referenced in these chapters.

To download your copy of the Strategy Driven for Success Toolbox, enter into your web browser the URL below.

http://www.valuegenerationpartners.com/downloads.html

Then, please complete and submit the download form. Thank you.

Introduction: Strategy Driven for Success

Strategy Driven for Success consists of applying processes and tools to define, deploy, execute, and achieve strategic goals and objectives. It may be applied at the corporate level, organizational, business unit, functional, or department level. Michael Porter, Harvard professor at The Institute for Strategy and Competitiveness, once said, "The best CEOs I know are teachers, and at the core of what they teach is strategy." All levels of successful leaders and managers apply strategic approach and methodology to ensure their organizations, customers, suppliers, and employees succeed.

This simple and comprehensive seven-step approach, called Strategy Driven for Success, may be applied in any industry or business – healthcare, construction, manufacturing, service, hospitality, non-profit, government, financial -- regardless of size.

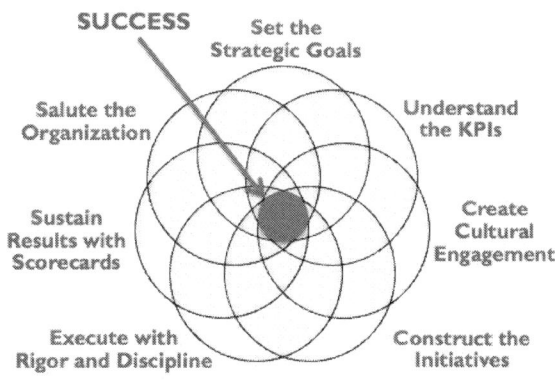

This handbook is designed for managers and leaders of all levels to define and deploy strategic goals and objectives. It combines the necessary elements of strategy definition and deployment into the following seven-step Strategy Driven for Success process:

1. **Set the Strategic Goals** – collect voice of... customer, business, employee, process, and competitor data; create organizational level SIPOCs; conduct SWOT analysis; draft SMART strategic goals and objectives; conduct force field analysis and refine strategic goals and objectives; define, communicate, and cascade strategy maps
2. **Understand the KPIs** – define, align, and cascade key performance indicators (KPIs) through the organization
3. **Create Cultural Engagement** – engage the culture with change leadership, conflict resolution, consensus building, motivating individuals, and team building

Introduction: Strategy Driven for Success

4. **Construct the Initiatives** – identify potential initiatives and projects, prioritize potential initiatives and projects, align initiatives and projects with strategic goals and objectives
5. **Execute with Rigor and Discipline** – execute the initiatives and projects to achieve the strategic goals and objectives using Project Management for Success, Problem Solving for Success, and/or Workshop Facilitation for Success
6. **Sustain Results with Scorecards** – define, align, and cascade KPI scorecards through the organization
7. **Salute the Organization** – recognize the organization, teams, and individuals – and celebrate success

Key to Strategy Driven for Success is timely, concise, and appropriate communication. George Bernard Shaw was quoted as saying, "The single biggest problem in communication is the illusion that it has taken place." As you execute the seven-step strategy-driven approach, ensure that in each step careful consideration is given to the impact on the many and various stakeholders and how that impact is communicated.

Benefits of timely and concise communication include:

- Understanding of strategic goals and objectives
- Facilitate support for the strategic goals and objectives
- Clarification of purpose, vision, mission, and core values
- Understanding and clarification of KPIs and scorecards
- Clarification of roles and responsibilities
- Status of the strategic initiatives and projects

We wish you much success in your pursuit of Strategy Driven for Success, thereby generating greater organizational value!

Introduction: Strategy Driven for Success

Define Purpose, Vision, Mission, and Values

Purpose, vision, mission, and values are critical for guiding your organization to successful achievement of strategic goals and objectives. These few statements and terms become key to an organization and culture, which is strategy driven for success. Each is defined and documented on the strategy map, which is communicated to the entire organization and made visible for reference and reminder on a daily basis.

Purpose Statement

A purpose statement defines why the organization exists and what it hopes to accomplish or change. It is a single sentence that conveys a message in terms of a result or outcome that changes and improves an existing condition.

W. Clement Stone is credited with the quote, "Definiteness of purpose is the starting point of all achievement." A purpose statement example might be written as; "The purpose of the quality department is to develop and deploy processes, procedures, and tools to increase quality and customer satisfaction."

Vision Statement

A vision statement describes where and what you want the organization to be in three to five years. It may be a single sentence or short paragraph that provides the organization with clear direction in terms of a summarized version of the strategic plan.

Jack Welch's perspective on having a vision is, "Good business leaders create a vision, articulate the vision, passionately own the vision, and relentlessly drive it to completion." A vision statement may be; "The vision of Southwest Health Systems is to reduce mortality rates from preventable diseases by becoming the number one provider of preventive healthcare in the tri-state area."

Mission Statement

A mission statement explains how the organization plans to achieve the purpose and vision. It describes the organization, how it operates,

Introduction: Strategy Driven for Success

the customers it serves, and the value it brings.

Stephen R. Covey is quoted as saying, "The principles you live by create the world you live in. So when you change the principles you live by, you can change your world. Your mission statement serves to summarize the principles you want to live by." An example mission statement is; "The mission of Software by Us is to employ qualified and satisfied employees who add value to our customers' businesses by providing high-quality and error-free software solutions that meet their total needs."

Core Values

An organization's core values are the foundational and fundamental beliefs and philosophies by which each employee should behave and perform. The core values serve to describe what the organization stands for, what it holds to be right, how employees will work together, and how its customer may expect to be treated.

Simon Mainwaring, branding consultant, social media expert, and advertising leader, describes the importance of core values as, "Define what your brand stands for, its core values and tone of voice, and then communicate consistently in those terms." Examples of core values include integrity, honesty, collaboration, innovation, loyalty, fairness, customer service, dependability, etc.

The purpose, vision, mission, and values are critical for guiding your organization to successful achievement of strategic goals and objectives. Define and document each of these critical elements on the organization's strategy map and communicate the strategy map to the entire organization. The strategy map – along with the purpose, vision, mission, and values – should be visible to the entire organization for reference and reminder on a daily basis.

Step One: Set the Strategic Goals

Step One of Strategy Driven for Success is Set the Strategic Goals. Clearly defined, communicated strategic goals and objectives are critical to the performance and success of an organization. A strategy map is an approach to define, document, communicate, and cascade the organization's strategies. It is a graphical diagram, which was presented by Robert S. Kaplan and David P. Norton in the mid 1990s, in association with the Balanced Scorecard.

Process to Set the Strategic Goals:

1. Assemble a team of participants who are briefed and come prepared to engage in the strategic goals and objectives session
2. Collect voice of... customer, business, employee, process, and competitor as input to SIPOC and SWOT analysis
3. Create organization-level SIPOCs with critical-to-customer (CTC) requirements as input to SWOT analysis
4. Conduct an organization SWOT analysis to draft strategic goals and objectives
5. Draft SMART strategic goals and objectives for each strategy map category
6. Conduct a force field analysis on drafted strategic goals and objectives
7. Refine strategic goals and objectives as necessary and appropriate
8. Define, communicate, train, and cascade strategy maps
9. Continue to Step Two: Understand the KPIs

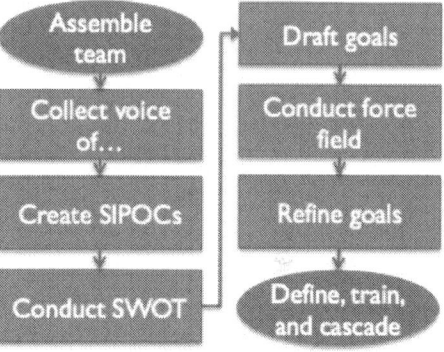

Set the Strategic Goals

Assemble team → Draft goals
↓ ↓
Collect voice of... → Conduct force field
↓ ↓
Create SIPOCs → Refine goals
↓ ↓
Conduct SWOT → Define, train, and cascade

Step One: Set the Strategic Goals

Collect Voice of... as input to SWOT Analysis

Understanding the voice of... customer, business, employee, process, and competitor is critical and necessary input to creating appropriate strategic goals and objectives. Each element provides information necessary for making informed decisions to identify strategies and lead the organization to success.

The following five categories are included in voice of... collection process:

1. Voice of Customer
2. Voice of Business
3. Voice of Employee
4. Voice of Process
5. Voice of Competitor

Benefits of collecting voice of... are many, including input to:

- Strategic planning process
- Identification and development of strategic goals and objectives
- Identification and development of key performance indicators (KPIs)
- Identification and development of scorecards
- Product and services offerings
- Pricing and service-level agreements (SLAs)
- Operational excellence initiatives
- Process improvement and continuous improvement initiatives
- Customer satisfaction initiatives
- Employee satisfaction initiatives
- Cultural transformation initiatives
- Organizational transformation initiatives
- Make-versus-buy decisions
- Budget planning process
- Expansion and capacity decisions
- Capital investment decisions

Step One: Set the Strategic Goals

Voice of Customer

Collecting voice of the customer information provides input and insights to your customers' current and potential needs, wishes, and expectations. It is a critical and necessary element of creating achievable and appropriate strategic goals and objectives.

Questions to consider when collecting voice of customer data:

- What is important to your customers?
- Who are your customers' customers?
- Where are your customers located?
- How do your customers use your products or services?
- What are your customers' sales levels and volumes?
- Is the customer a primary or secondary customer?
- Who else supplies your customers?
- What are your customers' strategic goals and objectives?
- What is your customer's financial position?

Methods of collecting voice of customer information may include:

- Scorecards and KPI charts
- Conducting telephone interviews
- Conducting face-to-face interviews
- Conducting surveys
- Conducting focus groups
- Reviewing customer sales levels and volumes
- Reviewing customer complaints
- Reviewing warranty data and service logs
- Interview customer service employees and associates
- Interview sales and marketing employees and associates

Voice of Customer Process

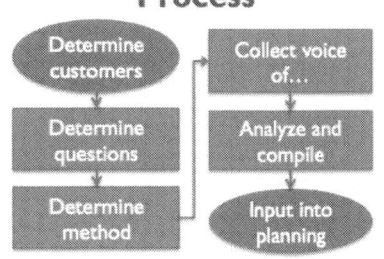

Voice of Customer Collection Process:

1. Identify target and key customers
2. Determine key questions to answer with voice of customer data
3. Determine method of collecting

7

Step One: Set the Strategic Goals

voice of customer data
4. Collect voice of customer data
5. Analyze and compile voice of customer data into results and reports
6. Input voice of customer into strategic planning process: SIPOC, SWOT analysis, SMART strategic goals and objectives, and Strategy Maps

Voice of Business

Collecting voice of the business data provides input and insights to your business's current and projected financial position. It is a critical and necessary element of creating achievable and appropriate strategic goals and objectives.

Questions to consider when collecting voice of business information:

- What are your market strengths and weaknesses?
- What are your current and projected sales volumes?
- What is your current and projected revenue?
- What is your current and projected profitability?
- What are your current and projected receivables?
- What are your current and projected payables?
- What are your current and projected margins?
- What are your current and projected liabilities?
- What is your current and planned budget performance?

Methods of collecting voice of business data may include:

- Scorecards and KPI charts
- Financial reports
- Budget reports
- Sales reports and projections
- Market analyses, reports, and projections

Voice of Business Collection Process:

1. Determine key questions to an-

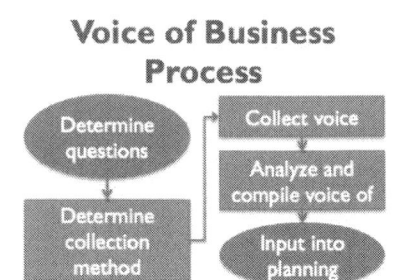

Voice of Business Process

Step One: Set the Strategic Goals

swer with voice of business data
2. Determine method of collecting voice of business data
3. Collect voice of business data
4. Analyze and compile voice of business data into results and reports
5. Input voice of business information into strategic planning process: SIPOC, SWOT analysis, SMART strategic goals and objectives, and Strategy Maps

Voice of Employee

Collecting voice of employee information provides input and insights to your business's culture and ability to execute strategies and initiatives. It is a critical and necessary element of creating achievable and appropriate strategic goals and objectives.

Questions to consider when collecting voice of employee data:

- What motivates employees?
- What are employee performance levels?
- Why do employees leave the business?
- What are employee productivity levels?
- Do employees understand how they contribute to the business's success?
- Do employees understand their roles and responsibilities?
- Do employees take ownership of company goals and objectives?
- Is the culture one of collaboration, teamwork, accountability, etc.?

Methods of collecting voice of employee information may include:

- Scorecards and KPI charts
- Employee satisfaction survey
- Employee culture survey
- Focus groups
- Performance appraisals
- Exit interviews

Voice of Employee Process

- Determine questions
- Collect voice
- Analyze and compile voice of
- Determine collection method
- Input into planning

Voice of Employee Collection Process:

1. Determine key questions to an-

Step One: Set the Strategic Goals

swer with voice of employee data
2. Determine method of collecting voice of employee data
3. Collect voice of employee data
4. Analyze and compile voice of employee data into results and reports
5. Input voice of employee data into strategic planning process: SIPOC, SWOT analysis, SMART strategic goals and objectives, and Strategy Maps

Voice of Process

Collecting voice of the process data provides input and insights to your business's current and projected capability, capacity, quality, cost, delivery, and performance levels. It is a critical and necessary element of creating achievable and appropriate strategic goals and objectives.

Questions to consider when collecting voice of process information:

- What are the key business processes?
- What are the current quality levels?
- What are the current rework and repair levels?
- What are the current delivery performance levels?
- What are the current cycle times?
- What are the current process issues?

Methods of collecting voice of process data may include:

- Scorecards and KPI charts
- Value stream maps
- Process maps
- Time tracking
- Employee interviews
- Data collection plans
- Customer feedback and complaints
- Quality and warranty records and reports
- Performance records and reports

Step One: Set the Strategic Goals

Voice of Process Collection Process:

1. Determine key processes
2. Determine key questions to answer with voice of process data
3. Determine method of collecting voice of process data
4. Collect voice of process data
5. Analyze and compile voice of process data into results and reports
6. Input voice of process data into strategic planning process: SIPOC, SWOT analysis, SMART strategic goals and objectives, and Strategy Maps

Voice of Process Process

- Determine processes
- Determine questions
- Determine method
- Collect voice of...
- Analyze and compile
- Input into planning

Voice of Competitor

Collecting voice of competitor data provides input and insights to your business's current and potential competitive profile. It is a critical and necessary element of creating achievable and appropriate strategic goals and objectives.

Questions to consider when collecting voice of competitor data:

- Who are your competitors?
- Who are your competitors' customers?
- What are your competitors' sales levels and volumes?
- What are your competitors' financial positions?
- What are your competitors' strategic goals and objectives?
- Where are your competitors located?
- What are your competitors' capabilities for products and services?

Methods of collecting voice of competitor data may include:

- Conduct market studies
- Review annual reports of competitors
- Review credit history of competitors
- Analyze competitors' products and services
- Interview/survey willing customers

Step One: Set the Strategic Goals

- Collect and review any publicly available information on competitors

Voice of Competitor Collection Process:

1. Identify current and potential competitors
2. Determine key questions to answer with voice of competitor data
3. Determine method of collecting voice of competitor data
4. Collect voice of competitor data
5. Analyze and compile voice of competitor data into results and reports
6. Input voice of competitor data into strategic planning process: SIPOC, SWOT analysis, SMART strategic goals and objectives, and Strategy Maps

Voice of Competitor Process

Determine competitors → Collect voice of...
↓ ↓
Determine questions → Analyze and compile
↓ ↓
Determine method → Input into planning

Create SIPOCs as Input to SWOT Analysis

SIPOC is a document summarizing a high-level process, including **S**uppliers, **I**nputs, **P**rocess, **O**utputs, and **C**ustomers. A completed SIPOC includes a list of the suppliers to the process, inputs to the process, the process itself, outputs of the process, and a list of customers of the process. Included in the SIPOC template is an additional column, titled "CTC," or Critical-To-Customer; it contains a list of the critical-to-customer characteristics expected *from* the process *by* the customer *of* the process. SIPOCs are useful and beneficial as input to the SWOT analysis for strategic planning.

SIPOC Documentation Process:

1. Assemble a cross-functional team of subject matter experts (SMEs)
2. Draw the SIPOC diagram or project the electronic template on a screen
3. Define the high-level process (beginning to end) in a few steps as a vertical block diagram in the process section of the SIPOC; the order in which the columns of the SIPOC template are completed

Step One: Set the Strategic Goals

    may vary depending on the team and the facilitator
4. Document the outputs from the process including materials, services, and information
5. Document the internal and external customers that receive the outputs of the process (customers may also be suppliers)
6. Document the inputs to the process including materials, services, and information
7. Document the internal and external suppliers of the inputs to the process (suppliers may also be customers)
8. Added to the traditional SIPOC are the critical-to-customer (CTC) characteristics expected from the process; the CTCs must be verified with customers of the process

SIPOC Documentation Process

- Assemble the team
- Create the SIPOC diagram
- Define the process
- Document the outputs
- Document the customers
- Document the inputs
- Document the suppliers
- Document CTCs

SIPOC is a powerful tool for identifying and documenting the complete list of process elements as input to collecting voice of... customer, business, employee, process, and competitor data and conducting SWOT analysis. A simple template, as depicted in the following image, will be helpful for developing a SIPOC for strategic planning purposes.

VALUE GENERATION PARTNERS — SIPOC

Facilitator:				Date:	
Process or Initiative:					
Suppliers	Inputs	Process	Outputs	Customers	CTCs

Conduct SWOT Analysis to Draft Strategic Goals

SWOT Analysis ... what a great tool to determine the **S**trengths, **W**eaknesses, **O**pportunities, and **T**hreats of your business, as input

Step One: Set the Strategic Goals

to identifying strategic goals and objectives! SWOT is often credited to Albert Humphrey of Stanford University, when, in the 1960s and 1970s, he led research projects using data from many top companies.

A SWOT analysis identifies internal characteristics and external elements that are significant to identifying, influencing, or achieving desired strategic goals and objectives. The SWOT analysis matrix is divided into two categories (Internal and External) and four elements (Strengths, Weaknesses, Opportunities, and Threats).

- **Internal** categories are *strengths* and *weaknesses*
    - **Strengths** are internal characteristics that will drive achievement of strategic goals and objectives
    - **Weaknesses** are internal characteristics that may prevent achievement of strategic goals and objectives, if not reinforced
- **External** elements are *opportunities* and *threats*
    - **Opportunities** are external elements that can be leveraged to achieve strategic goals and objectives
    - **Threats** are external elements that may prevent achieving strategic goals and objectives, if not mitigated

A SWOT analysis may be used as:

- A precursor to strategic planning and strategy map development
- Input to development of strategic goals and objectives
- A determination of strategic goals and objectives
- Input to transformational or operational excellence initiatives

Benefits of SWOT analysis include:

- Provide valuable input for strategic planning initiatives
- Proactive approach to determine which strategic plans and initiatives to undertake
- Provide a collaborative team environment
- Bring together diverse backgrounds and experiences

Step One: Set the Strategic Goals

Follow the steps below for a simple approach to conduct a SWOT analysis for determining strategic goals and objectives:

1. Assemble a cross-functional team who will be prepared for the session upon completing pre-work on the SWOT analysis topic: inputs to SWOT analysis are SIPOC; value stream maps; and voice of... customer, business, employee, process, and competitor data

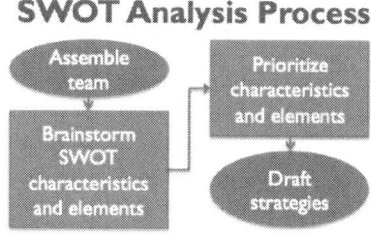

SWOT Analysis Process

2. Conduct the SWOT analysis by brainstorming a list of internal characteristics and external elements related to the strategic planning process
3. Prioritize the list – by category and element – for actions to leverage, mitigate, overcome, or exploit
    a. Map the strengths to opportunities, which can be leveraged, and to threats, which can be mitigated
    b. Understand weaknesses that need to be overcome to take advantage of opportunities, and that may be exploited by threats
4. Use the SWOT analysis results to draft strategic goals and objectives

SWOT analysis results are used to draft strategic goals and objectives. A simple matrix tool, as depicted in the following image, will be helpful for facilitating a SWOT analysis session to develop strategic goals and objectives.

Step One: Set the Strategic Goals

VALUE GENERATION PARTNERS **SWOT Analysis**			
Facilitator:		Date:	
SWOT Topic:			
Internal Strengths	**Score**	**Internal Weaknesses**	**Score**
External Opportunities	**Score**	**External Threats**	**Score**

Draft SMART Strategic Goals and Objectives

Using input from SIPOCs; voice of... customer, business, employee, process, and competitor data; and SWOT analysis, you may begin drafting strategies and defining SMART strategic goals and objectives. Other inputs to developing SMART strategies include value stream maps, impact/effort matrix, mind mapping, affinity diagram, brainstorming, etc.

Define and draft three to five strategic goals and objectives for each strategy map category.

- Financial
- Customer
- Internal process
- Learning and growth

Note that customized strategy maps may use variations of the four categories listed above. Strategic goals and objectives support and flow to the next higher category. For example, learning and growth strategies support internal process strategies, which support customer strategies, which support financial strategies.

Step One: Set the Strategic Goals

Developing SMART strategic goals and objectives is critical to Strategy Driven for Success. Without SMART strategic goals and objectives, the organization will have little chance of successfully achieving the strategies.

The use of SMART goals has been credited to Peter Drucker, through his management by objectives concept. The first-known writing of the term "SMART" occurs in the November 1981 issue of Management Review, in George T. Doran's article, "There's a S.M.A.R.T. Way to Write Management's Goals and Objectives."

Define SMART strategic goals and objectives by using the SMART Goal Definition and Statement template depicted in the following image. Then test it against the checklist to determine if it passes SMART goal criteria.

VALUE GENERATION PARTNERS — SMART Goal Definition and Statement

Facilitator:		Date:
Organization and location of goal		
Function and process of goal		
Current quality level of problem		
Desired quality level of goal		
Desired completion date of goal		

SMART Goal Statement:

Is the goal **Specific**?	Did you describe what process or outcome you plan to increase or decrease?	
Is the goal **Measurable**?	Did you list the current quality level and planned improvement level for when it is complete?	
Is the goal **Achievable**?	Did you base your planned quality level on facts and data?	
Is the goal **Relevant**?	Does your goal support the strategic initiatives of the organization and is it within your scope of influence and responsibility?	
Is the goal **Time-Bound**?	Did you list a date by which to achieve the improvement level?	

Once the SMART strategic goals and objectives are defined, transfer to the strategy map template in the following image for further analysis and refinement.

A simple template, as depicted in the following image, will be helpful for developing drafted strategic goals and objectives for further strategy map development.

Step One: Set the Strategic Goals

VALUE GENERATION PARTNERS	Strategy Map	
Business, Organization, Function, or Department:		
Facilitator:		Date:
Purpose:		
Vision:		
Mission:		
Financial		
Customer		
Internal Processes		
Learning and Growth		
Values:		

Conduct Force Field on Drafted Strategic Goals

Once strategies are drafted, conducting force field analysis on the draft strategies is a powerful technique to ensure the organization is set up for success. Kurt Lewin's 1940s Force Field Analysis is a very powerful, yet simple, tool to evaluate opposing forces (drivers and restrainers) and to determine actions for moving toward implementing a solution. The use of force field analysis has expanded over the years from its origins in social science to being used in a variety of business situations.

Force field analysis is a proactive approach to understand variables and forces around a particular strategic goal or objective, and to act on the variables in a positive manner.

Force field analysis may be used when:

- Strategic goals and objectives are being evaluated for viability
- Strategic goals and objectives are being evaluated for implementation
- There is concern for sustainability of strategic goals and objec-

Step One: Set the Strategic Goals

tives

Benefits of force field analysis include:

- Proactive approach to define and mitigate restraining forces that prevent successful achievement of strategic goals and objectives
- Provide a collaborative team environment
- Bring together diverse backgrounds and experiences

Force Field Analysis Process:

1. Assemble a cross-functional team of subject matter experts (SMEs) who will be prepared for the session as a result of completing pre-work on the topic
2. Construct a force field analysis diagram on a flipchart or use a template projected onto the screen
3. List the drafted strategic goals and objectives
4. List the driving forces, and rank forces from 1 to 5, with 5 being the strongest
5. List the restraining forces, and rank the forces from 1 to 5, with 5 being the strongest
6. Refine the drafted strategies, as necessary and appropriate, and/or define an action plan describing "who, what, and when" to leverage or strengthen drivers, and to mitigate or eliminate restrainers

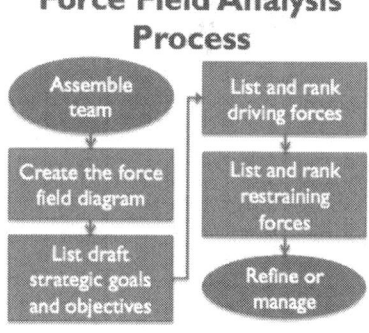

Note: Results from conducting a force field analysis on strategic goals and objectives shall be used as input to developing initiatives and projects to successfully achieve the strategic goals and objectives.

A simple matrix tool, as noted in the following image, will be helpful for facilitating a force field analysis session to evaluate strategic goals and objectives.

Step One: Set the Strategic Goals

VALUE GENERATION PARTNERS **Force Field Analysis**			
Facilitator:		Date:	
Goal or Solution Statement:			
List Drivers	Score	List Restrainers	Score
Total Driver Score	0	Total Restrainer Score	0

Define, Communicate, and Cascade Strategy Maps

Strategy maps may be developed and deployed – for a corporation, business, function, or department – to set and communicate strategic goals and objectives. It may be developed, then cascaded, from the top-level of an organization, with each subsequent level having a strategy map and scorecards supporting the next level up. Robert S. Kaplan said, "Process improvement programs are like teaching people *how* to fish. Strategy maps and scorecards teach people *where* to fish."

There are many approaches and options for defining and deploying strategies throughout the organization, such as Hoshin Kanri, Policy Deployment, Strategy Deployment, X-Matrix, or Strategy Maps. Strategy Driven for Success utilizes the strategy map approach to define, document, and deploy strategic goals and objectives.

Benefits of using a strategy map include:

- Provide an approach to ensure strategic goals and objectives are successful
- Provide input for selecting initiatives and projects to support strategic goals and objectives
- Provide input for developing balanced and cascading KPIs and scorecards
- Increase focus on the organization's strategies and attention on supporting metrics and KPIs
- Provide a consistent approach for defining, documenting, and communicating strategic goals and objectives

Step One: Set the Strategic Goals

Sections and supporting elements of a strategy map include:

Header

- **Purpose** – why the organization, corporation, business, function, or department exists
- **Vision** – where the organization, corporation, business, function, or department wants to be in the future
- **Mission** – how the organization, corporation, business, function, or department will work toward its vision

Body and Strategy Map Categories

- **Finance** strategic goals and objectives
- **Customer** strategic goals and objectives
- **Internal Processes** strategic goals and objectives
- **Learning and Growth** strategic goals and objectives

Note: Customized strategy maps may use variations of the four categories listed above. A lane or row on the strategy map is defined for each category, and each category will typically consist of three to five strategic goals and objectives. Strategic goals and objectives support and flow to the next higher lane on the strategy map. Strategic goals and objectives may cascade through the business or organization.

Footer

- **Values** – key and core values of the organization, corporation, business, function, or department

Strategy Map Process:

1. Assemble a team of participants who are briefed and come prepared to engage in strategy map development
2. Compile strategy map elements from previous work and inputs: purpose, vision, and mission; financial strategic goals and objectives; customer strategic goals and objectives; internal process

Strategy Map Process

Assemble team → Compile elements → Document strategy map → Communicate and train strategy map → Cascade strategy maps

Step One: Set the Strategic Goals

strategic goals and objectives; learning and growth strategic goals and objectives; and core values

3. Define and document sections and elements of the top-level business or organizational strategy map
4. Communicate and train top-level strategy map to the business or organization
5. Cascade strategy maps through each division, function, department, or unit within the business or organization by following the same or similar approach as the top-level map development process

The following example depicts a basic strategy map, along with its elements.

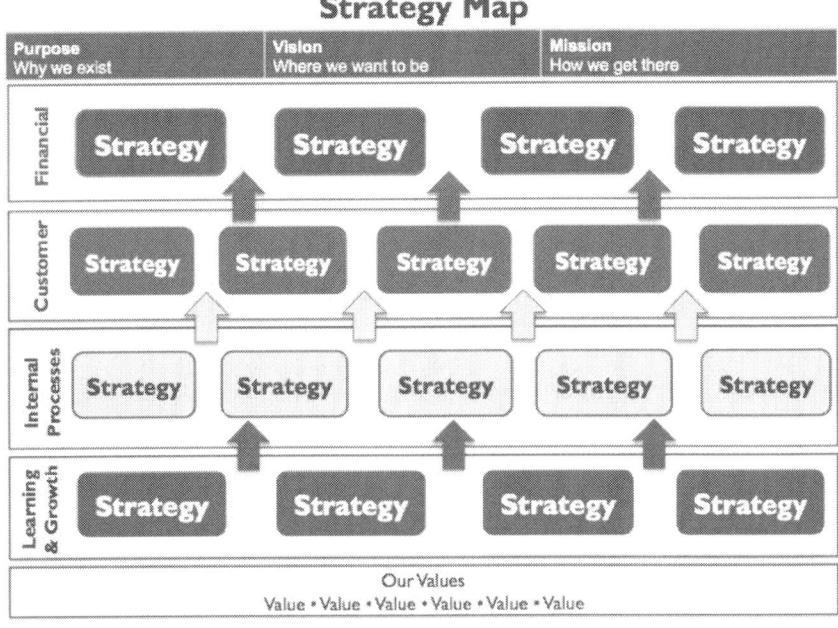

A strategy map is used as input to cascading and balanced scorecards and KPIs, as well as initiative and project selection and prioritization. While progress on strategic goals and objectives should be managed, measured, and communicated regularly, strategic goals and objectives should be reassessed, revised as appropriate, and communicated on an annual basis as part of the strategic planning process.

Step Two: Understand the KPIs

Step Two of Strategy Driven for Success is Understand the KPIs. From George Odiorne to Peter Drucker, the quote, "If you can't measure something, you can't manage it," has been discussed, spoken, and written in many forms over the years. Regardless of how the quote is written, you need Key Performance Indicators (KPIs) if you are to measure, manage, and achieve the strategic goals and objectives.

Process to Understand the KPIs:

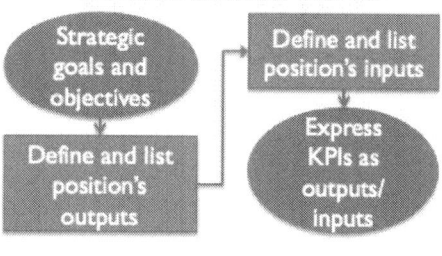

1. Start with the strategic goals and objectives for each level, role, or position in the organization
2. Define and list a position's outputs in terms of supporting the strategic goals and objectives
3. Define and list a position's inputs used to achieve the outputs
4. Express the position's KPIs in terms of outputs per inputs (see KPI examples in the following template)
5. Continue to Step Three: Create Cultural Engagement

The following template works well to identify and define KPIs.

VALUE GENERATION PARTNERS — KPI Development

Facilitator: Date:

Output	Input	Output per Input
Sales Closed	Sales Person	Sales Closed per Sales Person
Number of Cases Stocked	Employee	Number of Cases Stocked per Employee
Profit Dollars	Employee	Profit Dollars per Employee
Customers Satisfied	Customer Surveyed	Customer Satisfaction Percentage Level
Parts Produced	Employee	Parts Produced per Employee
Customers Serviced	Hour	Customers Serviced per Hour

This is the initial step in identifying KPIs, which will be further defined, developed, and cascaded through the entire organization with bal-

Step Two: Understand the KPIs

anced and cascading scorecards in Step Six: Sustain Results with Scorecards.

KPIs start with the top-level position in the organization (level one) and cascade through all subsequent levels. The top-level position has a KPI for each strategic goal and objective listed on the top-level strategy map. The focus of the KPIs is on measuring and managing the critical few business results as indicated by the strategic goals and objectives.

KPIs cascade through the organization to measure, monitor, manage, and achieve the defined strategic goals and objectives at each level. It is important to consider that what you measure drives specific behavior. Selecting a KPI that drives the wrong behavior may be much worse than having no KPI. Chuck Coonradt is well known for using cascading KPIs and scorecards in his methodology, "The Game of Work."

KPIs are balanced across the strategy map categories – financial, customer, internal processes, and learning and growth – to support strategic goals and objectives and to ensure focus is given across the critical areas of the business. Each KPI must be in alignment with vertical-level 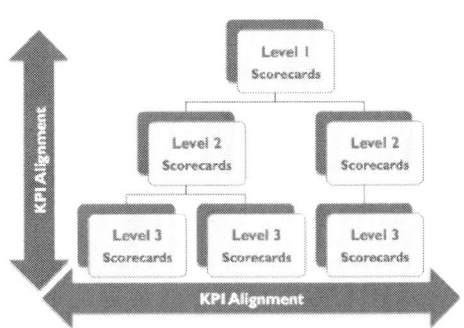 KPIs and horizontal-level KPIs, as depicted in the image. Each KPI level can take two to three months to define, deploy, and become part of the cultural norm. The number of KPIs necessary for each level and position is dependent on the level of the position and the position's direct impact on the strategic goals and objectives.

Benefits of Key Performance Indicators (KPIs) include:

- Support understanding of strategic goals and objectives
- Provide indicators of success and opportunities for improvement
- Allow for timely changes and adjustments based on results
- Measure individual performance and development opportunities
- Input for one-on-one sessions between managers and employees

Step Three: Create Cultural Engagement

Step Three of Strategy Driven for Success is Create Cultural Engagement. In this step, leadership, management, and the organization will apply approaches and techniques to engage the culture in successfully achieving strategic goals and objectives.

A useful and powerful approach to create cultural engagement is further defined in the **Cultural Engagement for Success Handbook** and summarized in the following the seven-step approach.

Step One: Set the Culture Strategy
Step Two: Understand the Current Culture
Step Three: Consider the Culture Gaps
Step Four: Create the Culture Plan
Step Five: Execute the Culture Plan
Step Six: Sustain Cultural Engagement
Step Seven: Salute Cultural Engagement

This section, Create Cultural Engagement, provides approaches and insights appropriate for engaging culture to successfully achieve strategic goals and initiatives.

Process to Create Cultural Engagement:

1. Lead change by facilitating cultural engagement toward the new strategic direction
2. Resolve conflict around current strategies and new strategic goals and objectives
3. Build consensus to gain full support for new strategic goals and objectives
4. Motivate individuals to achieve strategic goals and objectives
5. Build teams to execute initiatives and projects necessary to achieve strategic goals and objectives
6. Continue to Step Four: Construct the Initiatives

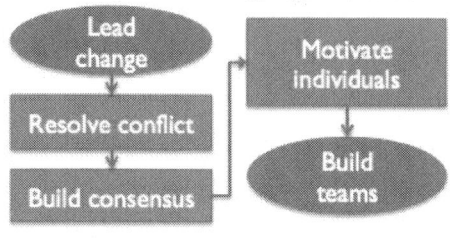

Process to Create Cultural Engagement

Step Three: Create Cultural Engagement

Change Leadership

Remaining competitive in today's global environment means organizations must be nimble and able to quickly implement new strategies and adapt to new strategic direction effectively. Changing a current-state organization to a desired, future-state organization requires solid competency in integrated change leadership. Change leadership is the act of leading and managing change; it is critical to the success of strategic goals and objectives, as well as to the overall health of a high-performance culture. Peter Drucker has been quoted as saying, "The greatest danger in times of turbulence is not the turbulence; it is to act with yesterday's logic."

Most strategic goals and objectives fail to deliver desired results due to the absence of many of these critical change leadership elements:

- Leadership support, involvement, visibility
- Focus on and commitment to the goals and objectives
- Clearly communicated and understood:
    o Purpose, vision, mission, and values
    o Goals, objectives, and expectations
    o Details and plans
    o Benefits and impacts to groups and individuals
- Sponsorship support at all phases of initiatives and projects necessary to achieve strategic goals and objectives
- Qualified, capable teams managing all aspects of initiatives and projects
- Application of project management, problem solving, and workshop facilitation rigor and discipline
- Availability of necessary human, financial, and technological resources
- Adoption plan with extensive organizational involvement
- Training and skill development plan
- Measuring and monitoring results
- Adjusting, as necessary
- Recognition and celebration of success

Considerations for leading change:

- Lead by example

Step Three: Create Cultural Engagement

- Communicate, communicate, communicate
- Balance needs of individuals with those of the organization
- Provide vision, direction, and focus, yet allow individual freedom
- Gain support for goals and objectives from all groups impacted and from all levels of leadership
- Monitor and measure the change; learn and adapt when problems arise
- The more complex the change, the more persistence and patience are required
- Don't bypass the change process
- Adjust approach based on the complexity of the change

Benefits of change leadership include:

- Improved organizational effectiveness, compliance, and risk prevention
- Environment of skill development, learning, and personal growth
- Sense of belonging and employee engagement
- Silos and barriers do not exist
- Better and more inclusive understanding of the organization and strategies
- Inclusive, collaborative environment in which individuals with diverse experience, skills, and backgrounds work toward common strategic goals and objectives

Depicted in the following image, you will notice three groups to consider during the change leadership process; they are:

- **Change leaders** – those who will assist in leading change because they perceive significant opportunity with little associated risk

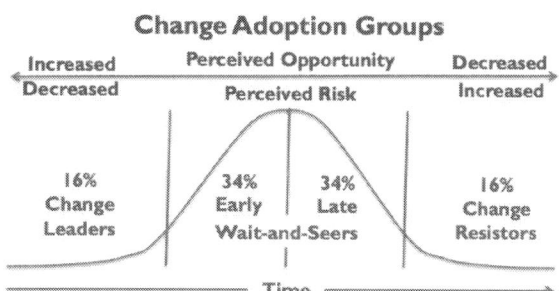

- **Wait-and-seers** – those who will change when they begin to see evidence that opportunity is increasing and risk is decreasing; this is the largest group of approximately 68 percent of individuals

Step Three: Create Cultural Engagement

- **Change resistors** – those who will resist change because they perceive little opportunity with significant risk

The change adoption curve defines phases, impact, feelings, and adjustments individuals and groups go through when faced with change. Based on work by psychiatrist and journalist Elisabeth Kübler-Ross, the change adoption curve depicts four phases, which are necessary to understand and manage when leading a successful change initiative.

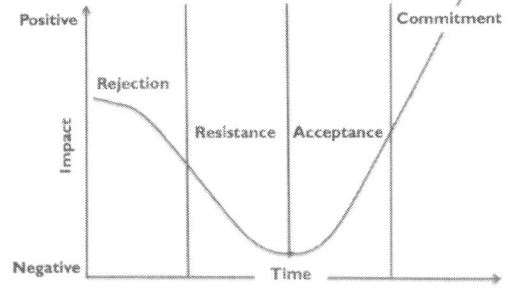

1. **Rejection** – "This does not apply to me and, if I wait, it will go away"
2. **Resistance** – "This won't work and I'm going back to doing it my way - the old way"
3. **Acceptance** – "This looks like it might work and may be even better than the old way"
4. **Commitment** – "This way works much better than the old way, and it's how I do things now"

The intent is to understand and use the change adoption curve, along with a change adoption plan, to reduce implementation time. Doing so will also reduce the change's negative impact on the organization and individuals. It is important to note that each of the three change adoption groups will experience the four phases at different paces, and with varying degrees of impact.

Change Leadership Process:

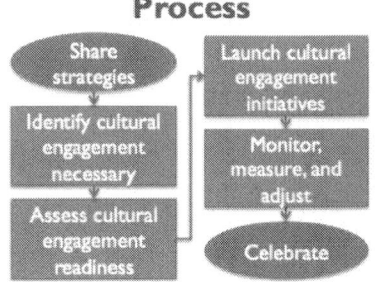

Change Leadership Process

1. Develop and communicate purpose, vision, mission, strategic goals and objectives, expectations, plans, and benefits
2. Identify cultural engagement necessary to support and achieve strategic goals and objectives

Step Three: Create Cultural Engagement

3. Assess and plan the organization's readiness for cultural engagement relative to strategic goals and objectives, using the following template

VALUE GENERATION PARTNERS — Change Readiness Plan

Change Initiative or Project Name:
Project Manager: Date:
Change Description:

Who	What		When	Other
Owner	Readiness Element	Required	Status	Date	Comments
	Leadership support, involvement, and visibility				
	Communication plan				
	Vision - communicated and understood				
	Reason - communicated and understood				
	Expectations - communicated and understood				
	Impact - communicated and understood				
	Benefits - communicated and understood				
	Sponsor				
	Charter				
	Approach				
	Initiative/project leader				
	Initiative/project team resources				
	Financial resources				
	Technical resources				
	Adoption plan				
	Training and skill development plan				
	Measurements for success				
	Other as appropriate				

4. Identify and launch cultural engagement initiatives to support and achieve strategic goals and objectives, using a change adoption plan as depicted in the following template

VALUE GENERATION PARTNERS — Change Adoption Plan

Change Initiative or Project Name: Project Manager:
Change Description:

Who			What		When	What	When	Other
Change Owner	Change Group	Stakeholder(s)	Resistance Level	Resistance Reason	Log Date	Adoption Strategy	Due Date	Adoption Status	Comments

5. Monitor, measure, and adjust the cultural engagement initiatives to ensure achievement of strategic goals and objectives
6. Acknowledge and celebrate success of cultural engagement that

Step Three: Create Cultural Engagement

enabled achievement of strategic goals and objectives

Not all change initiatives are equal in complexity, nor do they require the same level of process to implement. Change initiatives will vary from those that are "just do it," to those that are full organizational transformations. Use the process level necessary for successfully achieving strategic goals and objectives based on an analysis of its complexity and impact on the organization and individuals.

Conflict Resolution

Conflict around new strategic goals and objectives is natural and inevitable. Organizations are comprised of individuals from diverse backgrounds, with varying experiences, skills, goals, and opinions. Conflict results from differences in motivations and opinions, expressed by emotional responses, such as frustration, fear, anger, and excitement. Any healthy, successful, and sustainable culture has conflict; it is normal behavior. Wellness author and speaker Greg Anderson is quoted as saying, "The Law of Win/Win says, 'Let's not do it your way or my way; let's do it the best way'."

Benefits of healthy conflict resolution include:

- Provide a collaborative team environment
- Provide an environment where silos and barriers do not exist
- Increase focus and attention on achieving strategic goals and objectives
- Establish a culture where the expectation is to respectfully, constructively resolve issues
- Provide an inclusive environment in which individuals with diverse experience, skills, and backgrounds work together to achieve strategic goals and objectives

It is helpful to recognize symptoms of conflict, and more importantly, to determine and eliminate – or prevent – actual causes of conflict.

Symptoms of conflict include:

- Impatience with other team members
- Mistrust and lack of understanding
- Arguing; defending positions and ideas

Step Three: Create Cultural Engagement

- Ideas and suggestions are unconnected; not building on others' ideas and suggestions
- Distortion of facts and information to support personal agendas

Causes of conflict include:

- Threats to status and organizational structure
- Pressures from roles, responsibilities
- Differences in perceptions, values
- Differences in standards
- Clashes in motivations, behaviors
- Inconsistencies in priorities, goals
- Changes in processes, procedures

Considerations for preventing conflict:

- Appreciate limitations of arguing and debating
- Believe that ideas and solutions can be mutually acceptable
- Understand that conflict is a natural, healthy element of decision making
- Acknowledge that differences in ideas are useful and lead to creative solutions
- Openness to others' ideas and suggestions, with a willingness to examine possibilities
- Recognizing that some of the best ideas and solutions are generated through conflict resolution

Conflict Resolution Process:

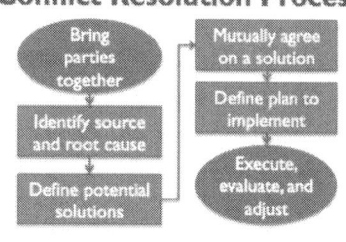

1. Bring together conflicting parties; select a comfortable and neutral environment
2. Identify conflict source and root cause
3. Define potential solutions to cause of conflict
4. Develop mutual agreement on an acceptable solution to the conflict
5. Define a plan to implement mutually agreed-upon solution
6. Execute, evaluate, and adjust the solution plan, as necessary

Conflict Resolution Process

Bring parties together → Identify source and root cause → Define potential solutions → Mutually agree on a solution → Define plan to implement → Execute, evaluate, and adjust

Step Three: Create Cultural Engagement

Considerations for resolving conflict:

- Encourage participants to propose and select the best solution
- Determine how important the issue is to all participants
- Listen carefully to each person's point of view
- Separate areas of agreement from disagreement
- Ensure all parties understand their responsibilities

Consensus Building

Building consensus is an essential behavior to integrate into the organization's culture; it is a key element ensuring strategic goals are supported and objectives are executed with ownership and accountability. Consensus building is the resolution of conflict and disagreement in order to reach a collaborative agreement with solidarity and harmony. It is a group decision and collective agreement, which is supported and carried forward by the group. Martin Luther King, Jr. is quoted as saying, "A genuine leader is not a searcher for consensus, but a molder of consensus."

Benefits of consensus building include:

- Provide a collaborative team environment
- Provide a consistent approach for making decisions
- Provide support and ownership of strategic goals and objectives
- Increase focus and attention on strategic goals and objectives

Consensus Building Process:

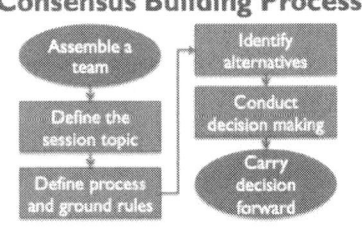

1. Assemble a team of participants who are briefed and come prepared to engage in the session
2. Define the topic, issue, problem of the session
3. Define session process and ground rules
4. Identify alternatives, such as solutions and options, to the session topic
5. Conduct decision-making process to formulate agreement and consensus
6. Carry the decision forward to the next step or phase

Step Three: Create Cultural Engagement

Elements of consensus building:

- It is not a win or lose situation
- Avoid debating and arguing over ideas
- Use ground rules established by the team
- State position with facts and respect
- Use proven facilitation tools and techniques
- Differences of opinion are natural and healthy; ensure they are stated in a respectful manner
- Involve the entire team in the decision-making process
- Ensure every member will support the decision
- No one leaves the session in silent disagreement

Tools and techniques useful for consensus building:

- Affinity diagram
- Brainstorming
- Force field analysis
- Impact/effort matrix
- Multivoting
- Nominal group technique
- Pairwise comparison

Thumbs up/down/sideways is a useful technique when facilitating a team through consensus building. It allows all of the members to participate in the decision in a visual manner, and it may lighten the mood and discussions during the process.

The "thumbs" approach goes as follows:

- Thumbs up – in complete agreement with the decision
- Thumbs down – in complete disagreement with the decision
- Thumbs sideways – not in total agreement, but will support the decision

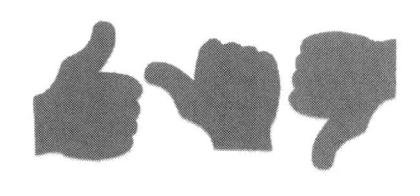

Consensus is reached when all team members have either thumbs up or thumbs sideways positions, and any thumbs down positions have been resolved.

Step Three: Create Cultural Engagement

Motivating Individuals

The most successful organizations are those that have a culture of motivated individuals who come together to form effective teams, accomplishing strategic goals and objectives set forth by the organization's leaders. And motivational leaders set the tone for such a culture. John Mackey, co-founder and co-CEO of Whole Foods Market, is quoted as saying, "If you are lucky enough to be someone's employer, then you have a moral obligation to make sure people do look forward to coming to work in the morning."

To motivate individuals, it is important to understand their needs. Effective leaders build and shape organizations that motivate their employees' minds, spirits, **and actions**. Cognitive evaluation theory (CET) of motivation indicates that there are two kinds of interconnected motivators to consider.

- **Intrinsic motivators** result from performance of an activity, including responsibility and achievement
- **Extrinsic motivators** result from environmental factors, including working conditions, pay, and performance evaluations

Intrinsic and extrinsic motivators are related to and impact each of these motivation theories.

- Alderfer's ERG Theory
- Herzberg's Two-Factor Theory
- Maslow's Hierarchy of Needs
- McClelland's Acquired Needs Theory

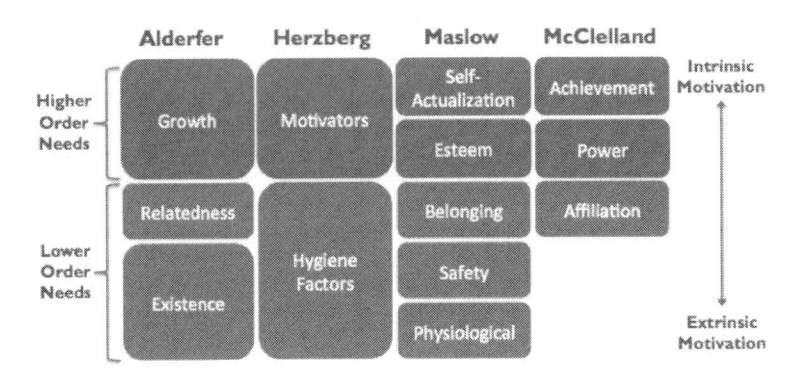

	Alderfer	Herzberg	Maslow	McClelland	
Higher Order Needs	Growth	Motivators	Self-Actualization	Achievement	Intrinsic Motivation
			Esteem	Power	
Lower Order Needs	Relatedness	Hygiene Factors	Belonging	Affiliation	
	Existence		Safety		
			Physiological		Extrinsic Motivation

Alderfer's ERG Theory:

Clayton Alderfer's ERG theory is formed on the basis of Maslow's Hierarchy of Needs, but collapses five levels into three categories – existence, relatedness, and growth.

- **Existence** – aspirations for material and physical well-being (includes Maslow's physiological and safety levels)
- **Relatedness** – aspirations for fulfilling relationships (includes Maslow's belonging and esteem levels)
- **Growth** – aspirations for development of capability, growth, or potential (includes Maslow's esteem and self-actualization levels)

Existence needs are considered the first level of needs and foundational to motivating behavior. As lower-level needs are satisfied, they become less important; as higher-level needs are satisfied, they become more important. To strive for a culture of motivation, leaders must ensure that individuals' lower-level needs are met (and thus no longer important), so that individuals have opportunities to achieve higher-level needs, such as relatedness and growth.

Herzberg's Two-Factor Theory:

Just as its name describes, Fredrick Herzberg's Two-Factor Theory is based on the premise that motivation is divided into two factors.

- **Hygiene factors** include job security, salary or pay, benefits, policies, relationships, and working conditions. While these factors do not directly motivate individuals, when not present or when taken away, they cause dissatisfaction and complaints.
- **Motivators** include achievement, advancement, growth, responsibility, and a feeling of recognition. When present, these factors directly motivate and satisfy individuals; however, when they are not present, they do not dissatisfy.

The two factors have four combinations:

- High hygiene and high motivation – best situation; results in individuals who have few complaints and are highly motivated
- High hygiene and low motivation – results in individuals who have few complaints, yet are not highly motivated

Step Three: Create Cultural Engagement

- Low hygiene and high motivation – results in individuals who are dissatisfied, yet highly motivated
- Low hygiene and low motivation – worst situation; results in individuals who are dissatisfied and not motivated

Since absence of hygiene factors causes dissatisfaction and complaints, and motivators cause satisfaction and high motivation, leaders must ensure that hygiene factors are in place, and then strengthen individuals' opportunities to experience motivators.

Maslow's Hierarchy of Needs:

Abraham Maslow's Hierarchy of Needs defines a need as a physiological or psychological deficiency requiring satisfaction. While a satisfied need is not a motivator, an unsatisfied need influences behavior until fulfilled.

Maslow's Hierarchy of Needs is based on two principles:

- **Deficit principle** states that a satisfied need does not motivate behavior since individuals work to satisfy missing needs
- **Progression principle** states that the five needs occur in a hierarchy, meaning lower-level needs must be satisfied first

Maslow's hierarchy consists of five levels:

- **Physiological** – workplace, work hours, comfort
- **Safety** – pay, work conditions, benefits, job security
- **Belonging** – coworkers, teams, leaders, customers
- **Esteem** – status, respect, responsibility, promotion, praise, recognition
- **Self-Actualization** – challenge, flexibility, achievement, growth, opportunity, advancement, creativity

Maslow's Hierarchy of Needs suggests that the lower-level needs must be met before individuals will desire moving to higher-level needs. Leaders must recognize and understand the five levels of needs in order to build a culture of motivation within their organizations.

McClelland's Acquired Needs Theory:

David McClelland's Acquired Needs Theory acknowledges that individuals prioritize three specific needs differently.

- **Affiliation** – wish to form close, personal, friendly relationships
- **Power** – desire to be in charge; to control and influence others' actions
- **Achievement** – determination to accomplish something of importance; to excel

Leaders must build and shape an organization that maximizes its results and success based on recognizing and meeting individuals' needs.

Benefits of motivating individuals include:

- Reduce costs and turnover
- Increase individuals' satisfaction
- Increase quality, productivity, customer satisfaction
- Provide an environment to ensure strategies are successful
- Provide a collaborative environment and sense of belonging
- Increase success of organization's strategies and metrics
- Increase focus, attention, energy toward organizational goals

Motivation Cycle:

1. Recognize an individual's deficiency of needs
2. Collaborate with individual to define a plan to fulfill his/her needs
3. Execute plan to fulfill needs
4. Monitor individual's motivation level
5. Provide feedback to/solicit input from individual; adjust plan as necessary

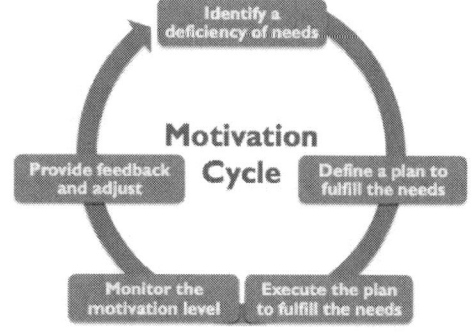

Step Three: Create Cultural Engagement

Although there is not a single, magical solution for motivating individuals, careful consideration of each of these theories and how they might be applied to build and shape a highly motivated organization will most certainly contribute to the successful achievement of strategic goals and objectives.

Team Building

Henry Ford, the founder of Ford Motor Company, delivered a clear and concise message regarding the importance of teams and the power of team building by saying, "Coming together is a beginning. Keeping together is progress. Working together is success." The strength and success of an organization's strategic goals and objectives are highly dependent on a strong team culture.

A team consists of people with complementary skills who are committed to a common purpose, with action plans and a set of performance goals for which it takes ownership and holds itself accountable. You may consider an entire organization a team, with an overall culture, and each department and function within the organization a team with its own subculture. You may also form teams with specific goals, purposes, and durations, as described below:

- **Ad hoc** teams are formed with short notice, for a specific purpose, with a limited scope and short duration, and may be comprised of cross-functional members
- **Cross-functional** teams are multi-disciplined and multi-functional, typically focused on efforts, processes, operations, procedures, and deliverables; they may cross multiple departments or functions
- **Functional** teams are permanent teams formed within a department to focus on specific functions within the organization
- **Improvement** teams address quality, efficiency, productivity, or transformational opportunities; they may be comprised of cross-functional members
- **Leadership** teams are formed to include those members of the organization who have a strategic role and guide the organization to achieve the vision, mission, and strategies
- **Project** teams work on specific initiatives that have defined deliverables, scope, and schedule to deliver a solution, such as a service, product, or other defined outcome; these teams may be

comprised of cross-functional members
- **Self-directed** teams are empowered to operate and authorized to deliver results without direction or supervision from management
- **Task forces** are comprised of experts with wide authority and decision-making freedom, formed for a specific purpose, which may be political or sensitive in nature; these teams may include cross-functional members
- **Virtual** teams are made up of members located in varying geographic locations; these teams use technological tools to interact, conduct meetings, and achieve goals

American industrialist and philanthropist Andrew Carnegie once said, "Teamwork is the ability to work together toward a common vision – the ability to direct individual accomplishments toward organizational objectives. It is the fuel that allows common people to attain uncommon results." Recognizing, understanding, and building on the stages of team development are critical to integrating a team culture into your organization. Psychologist Bruce Tuckman used the phrase "forming, storming, norming, and performing" in the article, Development Sequence in Small Groups, in 1965, to describe the process of group development in achieving high performance and delivering results.

Below are the four stages of team development:

Forming – members are typically excited, anxious, positive, and polite

- Have a strong dependency on the leader
- Starting to work together and get to know each other
- Feeling uncertain about their roles within the team
- Not yet sure what is expected of them nor what they may contribute
- Beginning to understand goals, deliverables, processes, and procedures

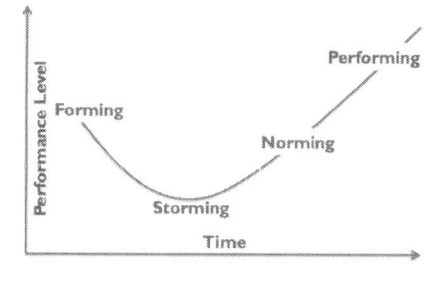

Step Three: Create Cultural Engagement

Note: As a leader of a team in the **forming** stage, your role is to provide clear and concise goals, objectives, and deliverables, and to provide the team with direction on roles and responsibilities. Encourage team members to have open dialogue and help members settle into their new assignments.

Storming – members begin to think individually, have conflict, are distracted from the goals

- Loyalties are divided; leadership is challenged
- Teams engage in confrontation, disagreements, arguments, complaining
- Split into sub-groups due to lack of trust for other members and/or leader
- Question the approach, methods, processes being used
- Challenge support for the team; may begin to rebel

Note: As a leader of a team in the **storming** stage, it is necessary to take on a more directive role in order to establish structure, clearly define how the team will work together, and clarify roles and responsibilities. It is your responsibility to build trust, resolve conflict, address concerns, and provide resolutions amenable to all members. You must recognize and address when members revisit the storming stage, typically due to membership changes, goals changing, or leadership changes.

Norming – members start working together, have less conflict, focus on the goals

- Goals, deliverables, and approach are understood and supported by members
- Understand and accept their roles and responsibilities, as well as others' roles and responsibilities
- Begin to work together as a cohesive team; trust and collaboration exist
- Focus is switched from conflict and challenge to achieving goals

Note: As a leader of a team in the **norming** stage, your role is to coordinate the team's functions and activities at a high level, and to guide the team to take responsibility and manage toward the goal.

Step Three: Create Cultural Engagement

Performing – members begin to focus on the process, operate efficiently, achieve goals

- Trust, positive energy, motivation, enthusiasm
- Ownership and clarity of the goals, approach, activities, tasks
- Exhibit open dialogue and communications
- Knowledgeable, competent, able to manage decision-making process
- Rely on each other; collaborative, interdependent cooperation
- Handle conflict; reach consensus

Note: As a leader of a team in the **performing** stage, your role is to delegate much of the authority and decision making to the team; focus your efforts on developing team members.

Adjourning is a fifth stage (for non-permanent teams), added by Tuckman in 1977, to identify when the work is complete and the team is dissolved. As a leader of a team in the adjourning stage, your role is to ensure team evaluations are complete, help members transition off the team and into another role, and celebrate the success of the team's accomplishments.

Benefits of building effective teams include:

- Environment of skill development and learning
- Approach for personal growth and satisfaction
- Collaborative environment; sense of belonging
- Environment where silos and barriers do not exist
- Inclusive understanding of the organization
- Environment to efficiently and effectively resolve issues that individuals alone cannot resolve
- Diverse and inclusive environment in which individuals work toward common goals

T Together
E Everyone
A Achieves
M More

Step Three: Create Cultural Engagement

Characteristics of a *successful* team include members having:

- An understanding of their roles and responsibilities
- An understanding of their purpose and goals, as well as a documented plan for how to achieve those goals
- Participation in team discussions and decisions, and to share accountability and ownership of execution and results
- Respect for each other and a commitment to resolve conflicts
- Appropriate communication and listening skills
- A use of fact-based decision making with data and statistical analysis
- Effective and efficient meetings, with adherence to ground rules and suitable record keeping

Leadership's contribution to a team's success includes:

- Provide sense of purpose and mission
- Provide plan and goals with direction and support
- Share business results
- Reinforce positive outcomes

Characteristics of an *ineffective* team include:

- Unclear goals and objectives, with no plan or little documentation
- Unclear roles and responsibilities
- Dominating members force their ideas on others
- Members' ideas are ignored and actions are limited
- Lack of involvement and communication
- Making decisions on instinctive reaction, with no facts or data to support
- Blame, unresolved conflict, lack of trust
- Tangents, digression, lack of focus

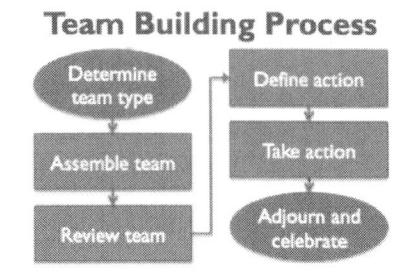

Team Building Process:

1. Determine the type of team required, based on the goals and objectives
2. Assemble and launch the team

Team Building Process

Determine team type → Define action → Take action → Adjourn and celebrate → Review team → Assemble team

Step Three: Create Cultural Engagement

3. Conduct reviews to identify the team's stage of development
4. Determine appropriate actions to move the team to performing stage
5. Take action with team until performing stage is achieved
6. Once team's goals are achieved, adjourn the team and celebrate its success

Step Four: Construct the Initiatives

Step Four of Strategy Driven for Success is Construct the Initiatives. Constructing the initiatives includes identifying, prioritizing, and aligning initiatives and projects with the strategic goals and objectives to ensure success.

Process to Construct the Initiatives:

1. Develop a list of potential initiatives and projects to support and execute the strategic goals and objectives; inputs to developing a list of potential initiatives and projects includes strategic goals and objectives, SIPOC, process maps, value stream maps, affinity diagram, and brainstorming
2. Prioritize the initiatives and projects with impact to the strategies, effort to execute, and risk if executed
3. Align the initiatives and projects with the strategic goals and objectives
4. Determine if gaps exist between the prioritized initiatives and projects and the strategic goals and objectives
5. Close any existing gaps with additional prioritized initiatives and projects
6. Continue to Step Five: Execute with Rigor and Discipline

It is a flow-down process from setting the strategies where the voice of… provides input to develop the strategy map with strategic goals and objectives. The strategic goals and objectives provides input to develop a hopper or list of potential initiatives and projects, which are filtered through a prioritization matrix to reduce the "trivial many" to the "critical few" that may be executed to achieve the strategic goals and objectives based on available resources of people, capital or budget, and time.

Step Four: Construct the Initiatives

The following image depicts the flow-down process from voice of... to strategy map, to "trivial many" initiatives and projects, to "critical few" initiatives and projects.

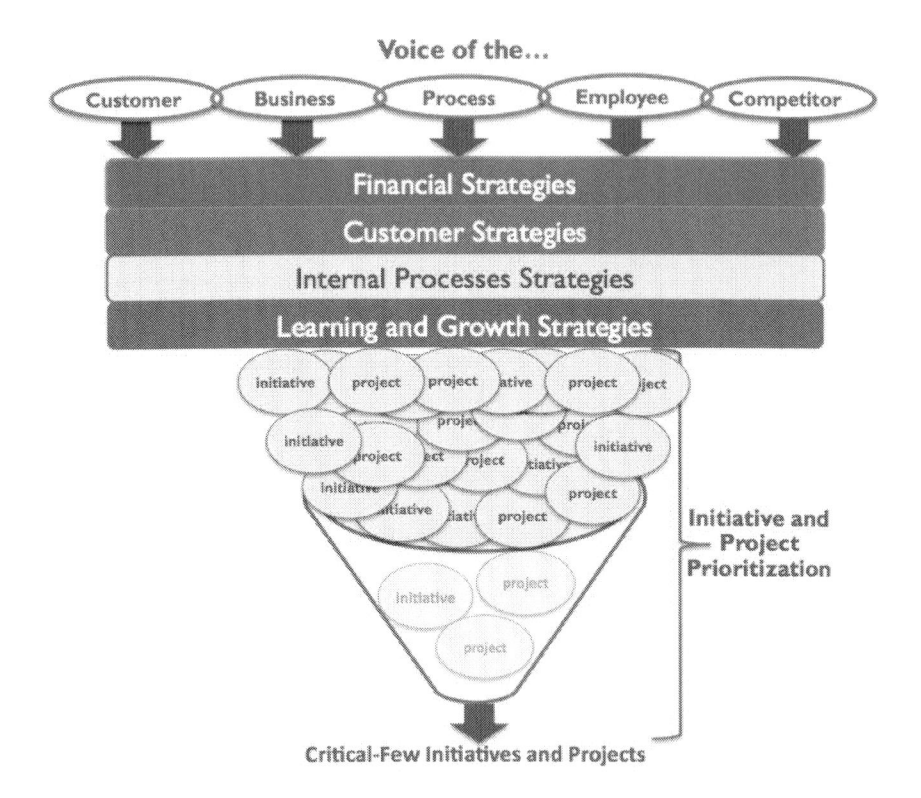

Identify Potential Initiatives and Projects

Once the strategic goals and objectives are determined, defined, communicated, and cascaded through the organization, the process of identifying potential initiatives and projects can begin. Resources such as employees, capital or budget, and time are limited. So while many potential initiatives and projects will be identified, not all will or can be executed. A prioritization process will be conducted to determine which initiatives and projects will be executed to ensure success of the strategic goals and objectives.

Step Four: Construct the Initiatives

Process to Identify Potential Initiatives and Projects:

1. Assemble a cross-functional team who will be prepared for the session upon completing pre-work review of the strategy map and strategic goals and objectives; inputs include strategy map, strategic goals and objectives, force field analysis, and voice of... results and reports
2. Create current-state (as is) SIPOCs for each strategic goal and objective
3. Create current-state process maps and/or value stream maps for each strategic goal and objective
4. Interrogate the current-state SIPOCs and process maps and/or value stream maps for issues, gaps, or risks preventing achievement of the strategic goals and objectives
5. Identify potential future-state initiatives and projects to achieve the strategic goals and objectives
6. Define SMART goals for each potential future-state initiative and project; use these SMART goals in the next step, which is prioritization

Prioritize Potential Initiatives and Projects

In today's fast-pace environment, resources and time are limited, and competition is fierce. Choosing the "right" initiatives and projects is crucial to the execution and achievement of the strategic goals and objectives. The flow-down process from strategic goals to the critical-few initiatives and projects is an excellent way to ensure that resources are working on the right things.

Benefits of prioritizing initiatives and projects include:

- Apply resources and efforts to top priority initiatives and projects
- Assure initiatives and projects support and impact strategic goals and objectives
- Apply resources and efforts to initiatives and projects with largest impact and least risk and effort

Step Four: Construct the Initiatives

Prioritizing potential initiatives and projects requires selection categories and criteria appropriate for the organization and the strategic plan. There are three typical selection categories for which to evaluate and prioritize potential initiatives and projects – impact, effort, and risk. Within the three selection categories are several selection criteria as defined in the following list and scoring scheme matrix:

- **Impact** to the strategic categories of finance, customer, internal processes, and learning and growth
- **Effort** by people, capital or budget, and duration of initiative or project
- **Risk** of technical needs and management needs within the initiative or project

The following matrix is an example of a scheme for scoring potential initiatives and projects to ensure successful achievement of strategic goals and objectives.

VALUE GENERATION PARTNERS — Initiative/Project Scoring Scheme

	Selection Criteria	Score 0	Score 1	Score 3	Score 5
Impact	Finance	No	Supports	Enables	Yes
	Customer	No	Supports	Enables	Yes
	Internal Processes	No	Supports	Enables	Yes
	Learning and Growth	No	Supports	Enables	Yes
Effort	People Resources		Low	Medium	High
	Capital or Budget Resources		In Plan	ROI	Out of Plan
	Duration of Initiative or Project		<4 Mths	>4<8 Mths	>8 Mths
Risk	Technical Risk within Initiative or Project		Low	Medium	High
	Management Risk within Initiative or Project		Low	Medium	High

Potential initiatives and projects are entered into a prioritization matrix for scoring and analysis. Each initiative and project is scored based on the categories of impact, effort, and risk and the associated criteria within the categories. An overall score and ranking is auto-calculated by the prioritization matrix. The scores and ranks can be sorted by largest to smallest to determine which initiatives and projects to move forward to the alignment matrix for gap analysis.

The highest ranked initiatives and projects are transferred to the alignment matrix to confirm no gaps exist between the initiatives and projects intended to achieve the strategic goals and objectives.

Step Four: Construct the Initiatives

The following matrix works well for determining prioritization of initiatives and projects to evaluate for alignment and gaps to strategic goals and objectives.

VALUE GENERATION PARTNERS — Initiative/Project Prioritization Matrix

Facilitator: Date:

#	Initiative/Project Description	Finance	Customer	Internal Processes	Learning and Growth	Total Impact	People Resources	Capital/Budget Resources	Duration of Initiative/Project	Total Effort	Technical Risk	Management Risk	Total Risk	Impact + Effort + Risk = Score	Rank
		25%	25%	25%	25%	100%	50%	20%	30%	100%	40%	60%	100%	Variable weightings	
1						0				0			0	0	0
2						0				0			0	0	0
3						0				0			0	0	0
4						0				0			0	0	0
5						0				0			0	0	0
6						0				0			0	0	0
7						0				0			0	0	0

Initiative/Project Prioritization Process:

1. Define the scoring scheme matrix with selection categories and criteria to be used in the prioritization matrix
2. Enter the list of initiatives and projects into the prioritization matrix
3. Score each initiative and project against the selection categories and criteria
4. Transfer highest ranked initiatives and projects to the alignment matrix in order to evaluate for gaps and to achieve the strategic goals and objectives

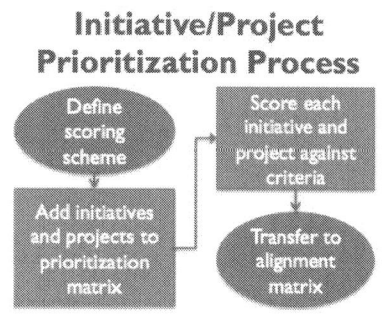

Initiative/Project Prioritization Process

Define scoring scheme → Score each initiative and project against criteria → Add initiatives and projects to prioritization matrix → Transfer to alignment matrix

Step Four: Construct the Initiatives

Align Prioritized Initiatives and Projects with Strategies

Now that the work of prioritizing the initiatives and projects is complete, it is time to align the initiatives and projects with the strategic goals and objectives. The alignment element is to determine if there are any gaps between the prioritized initiatives and projects to the strategic goals and objectives. If gaps exist, additional or different initiatives and projects must be selected to eliminate gaps and ensure successful achievement of the strategic goals and objectives.

Benefits of aligning initiatives and projects with strategic goals and objectives include:

- Ensure there are no gaps between initiatives and projects and the strategic goals and objectives
- Ensure initiatives and projects will successfully achieve strategic goals and objectives
- Confirm alignment with work being conducted (initiatives and projects) and expected outcomes being achieved (strategic goals and objectives)

Process to Align Initiatives/Projects to Strategic Goals and Objectives:

Initiatives to Strategies Alignment Process

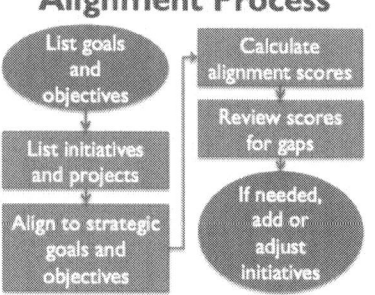

1. List the strategic goals and objectives (by category of finance, customer, internal processes, and learning and growth) across the top horizontal "X" axis of the alignment matrix
2. List the prioritized initiatives and projects down the left vertical "Y" axis of the alignment matrix
3. Correlate or align the initiatives and projects with the strategic goals and objectives with a numerical strength score of 1 for low, 5 medium, and 9 for high, or other scoring scheme of choice
4. The matrix will auto-calculate a total score for each initiative/project and each strategic goal and objective
5. Review the alignment matrix for strategic goals and objectives

Step Four: Construct the Initiatives

that do not have strong enough initiatives and projects to achieve success

6. If gaps exist, determine what adjustments or additional initiatives and projects should be included to successfully achieve the strategic goals and objectives by eliminating gaps

The following template works well to align and look for gaps between initiatives and projects and the strategic goals and objectives.

VALUE GENERATION PARTNERS — Initiative/Project to Strategy Alignment Matrix

Facilitator:												Date:	
		\multicolumn{12}{c}{**Strategies**}	
		\multicolumn{3}{c}{Finance}	\multicolumn{3}{c}{Customer}	\multicolumn{3}{c}{Internal Processes}	\multicolumn{3}{c}{Learning & Growth}	
		Strategy	Strategy	Strategy	Strategy	Strategy	Strategy	Strategy	Strategy	Strategy	Strategy	Strategy	Total Score
Initiatives/Programs/Projects	Initiative/Project												0
	Initiative/Project												0
	Initiative/Project												0
	Initiative/Project												0
	Initiative/Project												0
	Initiative/Project												0
	Initiative/Project												0
	Initiative/Project												0
	Initiative/Project												0
	Initiative/Project												0
	Initiative/Project												0
	Total Score	0	0	0	0	0	0	0	0	0	0	0	0

Step Five: Execute with Rigor and Discipline

Step Five of Strategy Driven for Success is Execute with Rigor and Discipline. Key elements of executing with rigor and discipline include using best practices in project management, problem solving, and workshop facilitation. This section describes these three approaches at a high level; further detail is available in the *Project Management for Success Handbook*, *Problem Solving for Success Handbook*, and *Workshop Facilitation for Success Handbook*.

Process to Execute with Rigor and Discipline:

1. Execute the initiatives and projects with rigor and discipline by applying one of the following:
    a. Project Management for Success is used to manage projects and teams to deliver a product, service, or improvement, as defined with strategic goals and objectives
        Step One: Set-up the Project
        Step Two: Understand the Requirements
        Step Three: Create the Team
        Step Four: Construct the Plan
        Step Five: Execute the Plan
        Step Six: Sign-off and Close the Project
        Step Seven: Salute the Team
    b. Problem Solving for Success is used to identify and solve problems by implementing sustainable solutions that support and enable strategic goals and objectives
        Step One: State Problem and Goal
        Step Two: Understand Current Condition
        Step Three: Conduct Root Cause Analysis
        Step Four: Construct Solutions
        Step Five: Execute Solutions
        Step Six: Sustain Solutions
        Step Seven: Salute the Team
    c. Workshop Facilitation for Success is used to manage and facilitate rapid improvement events designed to achieve strategic goals and objectives
        Step One: Set-up the Workshop Charter

Step Five: Execute with Rigor and Discipline

        Step Two: Understand the Logistics
        Step Three: Create the Team
        Step Four: Clarify Roles and Responsibilities
        Step Five: Execute the Workshop
        Step Six: Share Status of Workshop
        Step Seven: Salute the Team
2. Continue to Step Six: Sustain Results with Scorecards

Project Management (PM) for Success

Project Management for Success consists of applying processes, rigor, and discipline to achieve specific strategic deliverables and goals, as defined in the project charter and project plan. It includes managing resources and applying the knowledge and skills necessary to achieve strategic goals and deliverables within defined scope, schedule, and budget. Project management consists of managing a cross-functional, diverse project team – one in which members do not normally work together, do not have the same background or skill sets.

Projects are constrained by scope, schedule, and budget; they are launched to deliver a product, service, or improvement as defined by the strategic goals by adding value for the organization and customer. A project has a defined beginning and end, and is considered temporary in nature. A project is different from daily or routine operations, which consist of repetitive functions or activities.

This simple and comprehensive seven-step approach, called Project Management for Success, may be applied to any project in every industry – healthcare, construction, manufacturing, service, hospitality, non-profit, government, financial, etc.

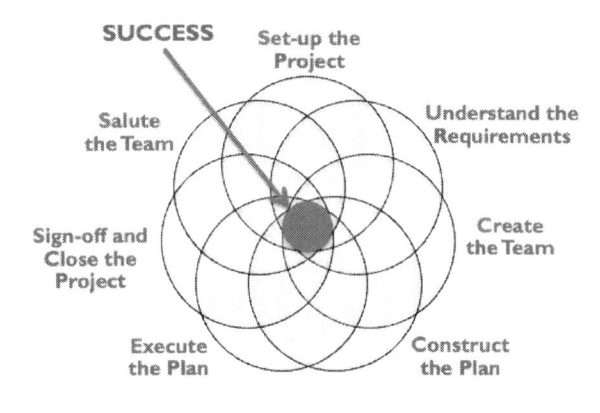

SUCCESS
- Set-up the Project
- Understand the Requirements
- Create the Team
- Construct the Plan
- Execute the Plan
- Sign-off and Close the Project
- Salute the Team

This approach is designed for project managers of all levels. It combines the best elements of project management processes and

Step Five: Execute with Rigor and Discipline

discipline into the following seven-step Project Management for Success process:

Project Management For Success

1. **Set-up the Project** – initiate toolbox; initiate checklist; create charter; initiate stakeholder management plan; initiate contact list; initiate communication management plan
2. **Understand the Requirements** – initiate requirements plan
3. **Create the Team** – initiate resource plan; update contact list; create RACI matrix; update communication management plan
4. **Construct the Plan** – construct work breakdown structure; create project schedule; initiate risk management plan; initiate change control plan; initiate issue management plan; initiate quality management plan; initiate procurement management plan; initiate financial reporting; update checklist; update resource plan; update stakeholder management plan; update communication management plan
5. **Execute the Plan** – use agendas, minutes, and status reports to manage, monitor, control, and report on project schedule and health, stakeholder management plan, project resource plan, communication management plan, change control plan, risk management plan, issue management plan, quality management plan, procurement management plan, financial reporting
6. **Sign-off and Close the Project** – complete the project checklist; close all open project plans; conduct lessons-learned session; conduct project sign-off and close
7. **Salute the Team** – recognize the team and celebrate success

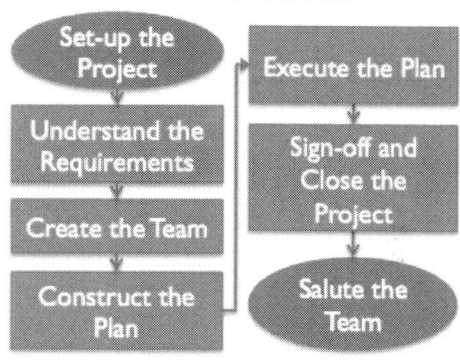

Benefits of using Project Management for Success processes and discipline to achieve strategic goals and objectives include:

- Improved quality and customer satisfaction
- Provide a collaborative team environment

Step Five: Execute with Rigor and Discipline

- Provide an approach for efficiently and effectively delivering results
- Increase focus and attention on maintaining scope, schedule, and budget
- Save cost and time by applying a methodical, disciplined approach to managing the project
- Provide a consistent approach for delivering the product, process, service, or improvement

Not all projects are created equal – in value or complexity, and not all projects require the same level of rigor. Generally, however, all projects will use and include some level of rigor until project completion or termination. The level of rigor applied is dependent on the complexity and value of the project. When complexity and value are minimal, you may wish to apply a more simple use of these steps; when complexity and value are at maximum, however, you will want to apply the full rigor and discipline of Project Management for Success.

Regardless of your project value, size, and complexity, you will want to consider these elements as you manage the project lifecycle:

- Create a project toolbox and checklist to manage your plans, templates, and artifacts
- Develop a project charter with clear scope, goals, deliverables, and metrics for success
- Understand, manage, and control your stakeholders
- Communicate, communicate, communicate
- Plan, form, develop, and manage your project team and resources
- Develop a project plan, schedule, action plan, and checklist
- Plan, manage, and control scope, schedule, and budget
- Analyze, plan, manage, and control issues, risks, and changes
- Plan, manage, and control quality and procurement
- Conduct status reports and updates
- Conduct lessons-learned session and project sign-off and close
- Recognize the team and celebrate its success!

Step Five: Execute with Rigor and Discipline

PM Step One: Set-up the Project

Step One of Project Management for Success is Set-up the Project. This step provides understanding and agreement with stakeholders regarding the project's deliverables and intended outcome. It is a vital starting point for the project team to understand, manage, and execute the project to successful completion.

Process to Set-up the Project:

1. Initiate the project toolbox with the templates and plans necessary to manage the project
2. Initiate the project checklist to manage ownership, due dates, and status of logs and plans used to manage the project
3. Create and secure approval for the project charter describing project goal, scope, deliverables, etc.
4. Initiate project contact list with names, email addresses, phone numbers, etc.
5. Initiate the stakeholder management plan with initial stakeholders and management plans
6. Initiate communication management plan with initial project communications
7. Continue to Step Two: Understand the Requirements

PM Step Two: Understand the Requirements

Step Two of Project Management for Success is Understand the Requirements. Software engineer and leader Steve McConnell is quoted as saying, "The most difficult part of requirements gathering is not the act of recording what the user wants; it is the exploratory development activity of helping users figure out what they want." A requirements plan is an essential tool to define and develop project requirements.

Process to Understand the Requirements:

1. Initiate the project requirements plan
2. Continue to Step Three: Create the Team

Step Five: Execute with Rigor and Discipline

PM Step Three: Create the Team

Step Three of Project Management for Success is Create the Team. Steve Case, entrepreneur, investor, and businessman, is quoted as saying, "You have to get along with people, but you also have to recognize that the strength of a team is different people with different perspectives and different personalities." What an important message to keep in mind when creating a project team.

Process to Create the Team:

1. Initiate project resource plan
2. Update project contact list with team members
3. Create a RACI matrix with team member roles and responsibilities
4. Update communication management plan with new team communications
5. Continue to Step Four: Construct the Plan

PM Step Four: Construct the Plan

Step Four of Project Management for Success is Construct the Plan. Albert Einstein is often credited with the quote, "If I had an hour to solve a problem, I'd spend 55 minutes thinking about the problem and 5 minutes thinking about solutions." While the quote may be found in many forms, the basic premise is always the same: Invest time up front to ensure a successful outcome.

Process to Construct the Plan:

1. Construct work breakdown structure
2. Create project schedule
3. Initiate risk management plan
4. Initiate change control plan
5. Initiate issue management plan
6. Initiate quality management plan
7. Initiate procurement management plan
8. Initiate financial reporting
9. Update checklist with new information on logs, tools, or plans
10. Update resource plan based on resource additions or changes
11. Update stakeholder management plan based on new information

and requirements
12. Update communication management plan with new communication requirements
13. Continue to Step Five: Execute the Plan

PM Step Five: Execute the Plan

Step Five of Project Management for Success is Execute the Plan. As quoted by Margaret Thatcher, "Plan your work today and every day, then work your plan."

In Step Five: Execute the Plan, the project team uses the toolbox, checklist, agendas, minutes, and status reports to manage, monitor, control, and report on the following:

- Project schedule and health
- Stakeholder management plan
- Project resource plan
- Communication management plan
- Change control plan
- Risk management plan
- Issue management plan
- Quality management plan
- Procurement management plan
- Financial reporting

Continue to Step Six: Sign-off and Close the Project when execution is complete.

PM Step Six: Sign-off and Close the Project

Step Six of Project Management for Success is Sign-off and Close the Project. It's when you validate that the *t*'s have been crossed, the *i*'s have been dotted, and you plan to recognize and celebrate the project team's success.

Process to Sign-off and Close the Project:

1. Complete the project checklist
2. Close all open project plans
3. Conduct lessons-learned session

Step Five: Execute with Rigor and Discipline

4. Conduct project sign-off and close meeting
5. Continue to Step Seven: Salute the Team

PM Step Seven: Salute the Team

Step Seven of Project Management for Success is Salute the Team. Key elements of this final step include 1) celebrating success of completing the project and 2) delivering required results, as well as 3) recognition of team members and their contributions.

Hilary Hinton "Zig" Ziglar was an author, salesman, and motivational speaker who once said, "Research indicates that employees have three prime needs: Interesting work, recognition for doing a good job, and being let in on things that are going on in the company." The strength and success of an organization's project management results are highly dependent on a strong team culture of working together and being recognized for successful results.

Process to Salute the Team:

1. Conduct the celebration and recognition event
2. Congratulate and release team members

Employing the seven-step process of Project Management for Success will result in successful execution of the project with certain delivery of the required results to meet the strategic goals and objectives.

Problem Solving (PS) for Success

Former Secretary of State, John Foster Dulles, is credited with the quote, "The measure of success is not whether you have a tough problem to deal with, but whether it is the same problem you had last year." Problems, also known as opportunities, issues, failures, defects, etc., come in many shapes and sizes and exist in every business and industry with varying levels of impact and complexity.

There are a variety of approaches, methodologies, and techniques to solve problems, including ISO Corrective Action, Ford 8D, A3 Thinking PDCA, Kepner-Tregoe®, Shainin®, and Lean Six Sigma DMAIC, to list a few. A simple, efficient, and effective approach to problem

Step Five: Execute with Rigor and Discipline

solving is one of the most lacking skills and sought-after competencies in business and industry today. Businesses need and want a simple approach to problem solving, one with predictable and sustainable solutions.

This simple seven-step, fact-based approach, called Problem Solving for Success, may be applied to any problem in any industry – healthcare, construction, manufacturing, service, hospitality, non-profit, government, financial, etc.

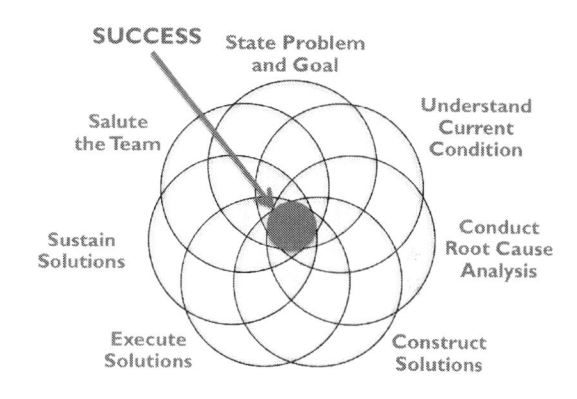

This guide to Problem Solving for Success is designed for problem solvers of all levels, regardless of their role, business, and industry. It combines the best elements of some of the simplest to most complex problem-solving approaches and methodologies into the following seven steps:

1. **State Problem and Goal** – initiate the A3 Problem Solving for Success Worksheet, document the theme of the problem, define the problem, and create a SMART goal
2. **Understand Current Condition** – document the current-state process flow
3. **Conduct Root Cause Analysis** – create a cause and effect diagram, list issues with the current state, analyze data, and conduct 5 Why
4. **Construct Solutions** – list potential solutions, analyze for impact and effort, pilot test and verify solutions, and define the future-state process flow
5. **Execute Solutions** – define and execute a solution implementation plan
6. **Sustain Solutions** – define and execute a solution sustainment plan, conduct sign-off, and close the problem-solving effort
7. **Salute the Team** – recognize the team and celebrate success

Step Five: Execute with Rigor and Discipline

Employing the seven-step process of Problem Solving for Success will result in a solution that solves the problem and sustains the results. The ensuing sections and chapters provide detail and information necessary to apply the seven-step Problem Solving for Success approach to every problem of any size and complexity for every industry and business.

Based on the complexity, time restrictions, resource availability, organizational goals and needs, etc., Problem Solving for Success may be conducted with one of two approaches. Problem solving may be conducted as a project-oriented approach as described in the seven-step Problem Solving for Success process sections of this handbook. Or, problem solving may be conducted in a condensed, event-based approach, as described in the Rapid Problem Solving for Success section toward the back of the handbook.

The A3 Problem Solving for Success Worksheet, found in the *Problem Solving for Success Toolbox,* is used to guide problem-solving efforts. It is a variation of an A3 Thinking PDCA template, and it is used to document, summarize, and report problem-solving progress and status.

VALUE GENERATION PARTNERS	A3 - Problem Solving for Success Worksheet			
Theme:		Potential Solutions	Impact	Effort
Problem Solver: Date:				
Problem Statement: no names, no solutions, list roles/functions, location, when, quantity, and cost				
SMART Goal: Specific – Measurable – Achievable – Relevant – Time-Bound:				
		Future State Process:		
Current State Process:				
		Actions to Implement the Solution	Who	When
Cause and Effect Diagram or List of Issues with Current State:				
		Actions necessary to Sustain the Solution	Who	When
Root Cause: why the problem occurred, was not detected, and was not prevented				
Why 1:				
Why 2:				
Why 3:		Sign-off		Date
Why 4:				
Why 5:				

PS Step One: State Problem and Goal

Step One of Problem Solving for Success is State Problem and Goal.

Step Five: Execute with Rigor and Discipline

In this step, the problem solver initiates an A3 Problem Solving for Success Worksheet by entering the theme of the problem, the problem statement, and a SMART goal representative of the problem.

Theme:	
Problem Solver:	Date:
Problem Statement: no names, no solutions; list roles/functions, location, when, quantity, and cost:	
SMART Goal: Specific – Measurable – Achievable – Relevant – Time-Bound:	

PS Step Two: Understand Current Condition

Step Two of Problem Solving for Success is Understand Current Condition. W. Edwards Deming is credited with the phrase, "If you can't describe what you are doing as a process, you don't know what you're doing."

In this step, the problem solver documents the current-state process flow on the A3 Problem Solving for Success Worksheet.

Current State Process:

PS Step Three: Conduct Root Cause Analysis

Step Three of Problem Solving for Success is Conduct Root Cause Analysis. This step involves determining the true root cause of the problem statement developed in Step One: State Problem and Goal. Naoto Kan, former Prime Minister of Japan, is quoted as saying, "If you are unable to understand the cause of a problem, it is impossible to solve it."

Step Five: Execute with Rigor and Discipline

In this step, the problem solver documents the cause and effect diagram and 5 Why root cause analysis on the A3 Problem Solving for Success Worksheet.

Cause and Effect Diagram or List of Issues with Current State:
Root Cause: why the problem occurred, was not detected, and was not prevented
Why 1:
Why 2:
Why 3:
Why 4:
Why 5:

PS Step Four: Construct Solutions

Step Four of Problem Solving for Success is Construct Solutions. Tony Robbins is quoted as saying, "Identify your problems, but give your power and energy to solutions." This section describes the approach for identifying solutions and the process for selecting solutions that, when implemented, will eliminate the root cause and sustain results.

In this step, the problem solver documents solution selection and the future-state process on the A3 Problem Solving for Success Worksheet.

Step Five: Execute with Rigor and Discipline

Potential Solutions	Impact	Effort

Future State Process:

PS Step Five: Execute Solutions

Step Five of Problem Solving for Success is Execute Solutions. As quoted by Tom Landry, "Setting a goal is not the main thing. It is deciding how you will go about achieving it and staying with that plan." The action plan to implement the solution is the tool to execute sustainable solutions.

In this step, the problem solver documents and executes actions to implement the solution.

Actions to Implement the Solution	Who	When

Process to Execute Solutions:

1. Define and document actions necessary to implement the solution; inputs to a solution implementation plan include details and results from the previous problem-solving step – Construct Solutions
2. Assign ownership of each action

Step Five: Execute with Rigor and Discipline

3. Determine and document due dates for each action
4. Monitor the status of each action and implement countermeasures if an action due date is at risk, behind schedule, or not delivering the desired results
5. Add actions to the implementation plan, as necessary

PS Step Six: Sustain Solutions

Step Six of Problem Solving for Success is Sustain Solutions. Henry Ford is quoted as saying, "If you think you can or you think you can't, you're right." The solution sustainment plan is the tool to succeed with a sustainable solution.

In this step, the problem solver documents and executes actions necessary to sustain the solution. Sign-off on the A3 Problem Solving for Success Worksheet is secured upon verification of solution sustainment.

Actions necessary to Sustain the Solution	Who	When
Sign-off		Date

Process to Sustain Solutions:

1. Define and document actions necessary to sustain the solution; inputs to a solution sustainment plan include details and results from the previous problem-solving steps – Conduct Root Cause Analysis, Construct Solutions, and Execute Solutions
2. Assign ownership of each action
3. Determine and document due dates for each action
4. Monitor the status each action and implement countermeasures, if an action is late or not delivering the desired results
5. Add actions to the sustainment plan, as necessary
6. Conduct training on the solution
7. Verify sustainment of the solution
8. Close and hand-off the solution

Step Five: Execute with Rigor and Discipline

PS Step Seven: Salute the Team

Step Seven of Problem Solving for Success is Salute the Team. Key elements of this final step include 1) celebrating success of solving the problem and 2) sustaining the solution, as well as 3) recognition of team members and their contributions.

Henry Ford, the founder of Ford Motor Company, delivered a clear and concise message regarding the importance of teams and the power of team building by saying, "Coming together is a beginning. Keeping together is progress. Working together is success." The strength and success of an organization's problem-solving efforts are highly dependent on a strong team culture.

Employing the seven-step process of Problem Solving for Success results in solving problems with sustainable solutions, which successfully achieve the strategic goals and objectives.

Workshop Facilitation (WF) for Success

Workshop Facilitation for Success is an efficient and effective approach to managing and achieving strategic goals and objectives in a face-to-face, cross-functional environment. Workshop facilitation may be conducted as one-day to five-day events to achieve strategic goals and objectives based on many purposes, such as process improvement, waste reduction, cost-of-quality reduction, project selection, and strategy development and deployment. Much thought and consideration must be given to planning and conducting workshop facilitation to ensure successful outcomes.

Workshop facilitation may be useful when:

- There are many and varying opinions on how to achieve strategic goals and objectives
- Strategic goals and objectives must be completed in a short cycle time
- Team and cross-functional collaboration are necessary to ensure success of strategic goals and objectives
- It is necessary for a group to work in a face-to-face environment to achieve strategic goals and objectives
- Strategic goals and objectives include waste reduction, cycle-time

Step Five: Execute with Rigor and Discipline

reduction, process improvement, or quality improvement

This simple seven-step approach, called Workshop Facilitation for Success, may be applied to achieve strategic goals and objectives in any industry – healthcare, construction, manufacturing, service, hospitality, non-profit, government, financial, etc. Workshop Facilitation for Success is designed for facilitators of all levels, regardless of their role, business, and industry. It combines the most effective and efficient elements of workshop facilitation approaches into the following seven steps:

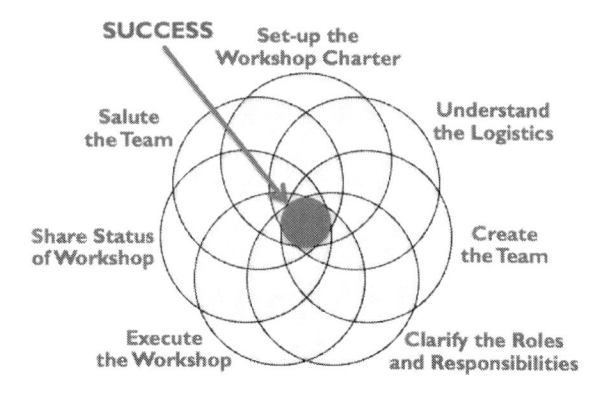

1. **Set-up the Workshop Charter** – define, develop, and approve a workshop charter that outlines the workshop description, clear goals, deliverables, objectives, in/out of scope, success criteria, and timeline for completion
2. **Understand the Logistics** – determine the workshop budget, where and when it will be conducted, and the duration of the workshop
3. **Create the Team** – identify participants and experience required to conduct the workshop and achieve the goals and objectives
4. **Clarify Roles and Responsibilities** – conduct a workshop kick-off call with the participants to describe workshop purpose, goals, and deliverables; roles and responsibilities before, during, and after the workshop; provide participants with pre-work assignments
5. **Execute the Workshop** – conduct the workshop using a defined agenda, along with tools and techniques as described in the facilitator's toolbox section of this handbook, to manage through a full and clear understanding of current-state (as is) condition and defining future-state (to be) condition, along with an executable action plan
6. **Share Status of Workshop** – conduct report-out at the conclusion of the workshop, then conduct ongoing status reporting post workshop until all action items are complete

Step Five: Execute with Rigor and Discipline

7. **Salute the Team** – recognize the team and celebrate success

Benefits of workshop facilitation include:

- Provide a collaborative team environment
- Provide a consistent approach for facilitating workshops
- Increase focus and attention on goals and objectives
- Save cost and time through rapid goal and objective achievement
- Provide an efficient and effective approach for achieving goals and objectives

WF Step One: Set-up the Workshop Charter

Step One of Workshop Facilitation for Success is Set-up the Workshop Charter using the following process:

1. Identify facilitator, sponsor, and key stakeholders
2. Facilitator and sponsor develop workshop charter: workshop description; SMART strategic goals, objectives, deliverables; timeline for completion of strategic deliverables; in-scope and out-of-scope statements; success criteria, metrics, and KPIs; issues, risks, dependencies
3. Continue to Step Two: Understand the Logistics

WF Step Two: Understand the Logistics

Step Two of Workshop Facilitation for Success is Understand the Logistics using the following process:

1. Facilitator and sponsor determine workshop budget for travel, location, snacks, lunches, etc.
2. Facilitator and sponsor determine the workshop date, location, and duration; ideally the participants are provided two to four weeks to prepare for the workshop topic and schedule
3. Facilitator secures workshop location and supplies: butcher block paper, flip charts, Post-it® notes, markers, tape, digital projector, etc.
4. Facilitator plans to arrive at the workshop location in advance to ensure appropriate set-up and preparation: u-shape room arrangement, refreshments (water, coffee, snacks, etc.), event supplies, etc.

Step Five: Execute with Rigor and Discipline

5. Continue to Step Three: Create the Team

WF Step Three: Create the Team

Babe Ruth is quoted as saying, "The way a team plays as a whole determines its success. You may have the greatest bunch of individual stars in the world, but if they don't play together, the club won't be worth a dime." Step Three of Workshop Facilitation for Success is Create the Team using the following process:

1. Facilitator and sponsor identify workshop participants and expertise required based on strategic goals and objectives: subject matter experts (SMEs), decision-making support, analytical support, technical support, documentation support, etc.
2. Continue to Step Four: Clarify Roles and Responsibilities

WF Step Four: Clarify Roles and Responsibilities

Step Four of Workshop Facilitation for Success is Clarify Roles and Responsibilities using the following process:

1. Facilitator and sponsor conduct a kick-off call/meeting with workshop participants to describe: workshop purpose and deliverables based on strategic goals and objectives; participants' roles and responsibilities for before, during, and after the event; preparation and pre-work
2. Facilitator provides participants with pre-work on the workshop topic
3. Continue to Step Five: Execute the Workshop

WF Step Five: Execute the Workshop

Step Five of Workshop Facilitation for Success is Execute the Workshop using the following process:

1. Sponsor and facilitator kick-off the workshop: strategic goals, objectives, scope, etc.; introductions, expectations, concerns, ground rules; participant roles and responsibilities; agenda items, time, duration; facilities, snacks, lunches, etc.
2. Participants define and document the current (as is) condition as it relates to the strategic goals and objectives; may develop a

Step Five: Execute with Rigor and Discipline

    SIPOC, RACI, flowchart, input/output map, or deployment flowchart; may conduct a SWOT analysis
3. Participants list issues within the current condition that prevent achievement of the strategic goals and objectives; may conduct silent brainstorming, create an affinity diagram, or facilitate mind mapping
4. Participants prioritize issues with current condition; may use multi-voting or pairwise comparison
5. Participants determine the cause of the prioritized issues; may use cause-and-effect diagram, cause-and-effect matrix, and 5 Why
6. Participants define and document a future-state (ideal) condition, which achieves the strategic goals and objectives; may develop a SIPOC, RACI, flowchart, input/output map, or deployment flowchart; may use solution-selection matrix or Pugh matrix; may create an impact/effort matrix or force field analysis; may conduct FMEA
7. Participants define a workshop action plan to implement the future-state condition, which achieves the strategic goals and objectives
8. Identify owner(s) of the workshop action plan items
9. Identify a workshop action plan implementation team – who, what, and when; define a close-out plan and timeline; workshop action items should be planned and managed to be completed within 30 days of the workshop and no longer than 90 days; define a communication plan, training plan, and control plan
10. Continue to Step Six: Share Status of Workshop

WF Step Six: Share Status of Workshop

Step Six of Workshop Facilitation for Success is Share Status of Workshop using the following process:

1. Participants conduct a workshop status report-out at the end of the workshop with the sponsor and key stakeholders; participants, not the facilitator, present the workshop status report-out; secure approval to proceed with the workshop action plan
2. Workshop action plan owner conducts weekly team update calls on managing the action plan assignments until completion; workshop action items should be managed to be completed within 30 days of the workshop and no longer than 90 days

Step Five: Execute with Rigor and Discipline

3. Workshop action plan owner and team conduct sponsor updates based on the communication plan
4. Workshop action plan owner conducts a close-out call with the sponsor when all workshop action items are complete
5. Continue to Step Seven: Salute the Team

WF Step Seven: Salute the Team

Poet Senora Roy once said, "We can accomplish more together than we would dream possible working by ourselves." Recognizing the team's success and contributions is key to future workshops' abilities to deliver planned and expected results. Step Seven of Workshop Facilitation for Success is Salute the Team using the following process:

1. Facilitator, action plan owner, and sponsor conduct team recognition and action plan close-out celebration

Employing the seven-step process of Workshop Facilitation for Success results in rapid and successful execution of strategic goals and objectives.

Step Six: Sustain Results with Scorecards

Step Six of Strategy Driven for Success is Sustain Results with Scorecards. Chuck Coonradt is well known for using cascading scorecards in his methodology, "The Game of Work." Robert Kaplan and David Norton are authors of "The Balanced Scorecard" and are credited with the balanced scorecard concept.

Scorecards are the graphical representation and the management of the KPIs defined in Step Two: Understand the KPIs. Each defined KPI shall have a scorecard to measure, monitor, and manage progress toward achieving and improving upon the strategic goals and objectives. While Step Two was the initial development of the KPIs to align with the strategic goals and objectives, additional definition of KPIs may take place in this step as the scorecards are developed and cascaded throughout the organization.

Process to Sustain Results with Scorecards:

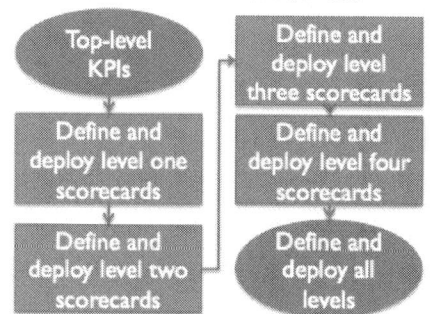

1. Start with top-level KPIs
2. Work with level one leader to define scorecards for each KPI to achieve organization's strategic goals and objectives
3. Deploy level one scorecards making them understood and visible to the entire organization
4. Work with direct reports of the level one leader, along with level one leader, to define scorecards for each KPI to achieve level two strategic goals and objectives that are aligned with the organization's strategic goals and objectives
5. Deploy level two scorecards making them clearly understood and visible to the entire organization
6. Continue to define and deploy scorecards for each level and position in the organization, ensuring vertical and horizontal KPI alignment to strategic goals and objects; deployment of KPIs at each level may take two to three months
7. Continue to Step Seven: Salute the Organization

Step Six: Sustain Results with Scorecards

Balanced and Cascading Scorecards

Balanced and cascading scorecards are necessary to achieve the strategic goals and initiatives. Scorecards start with plotting the KPIs of the top-level position in the organization and cascading through all subsequent levels. The focus is on measuring, monitoring, and managing the critical few business results as defined with the strategic goals and objectives. Each scorecard must be in alignment with vertical-level scorecards and the horizontal-level scorecards.

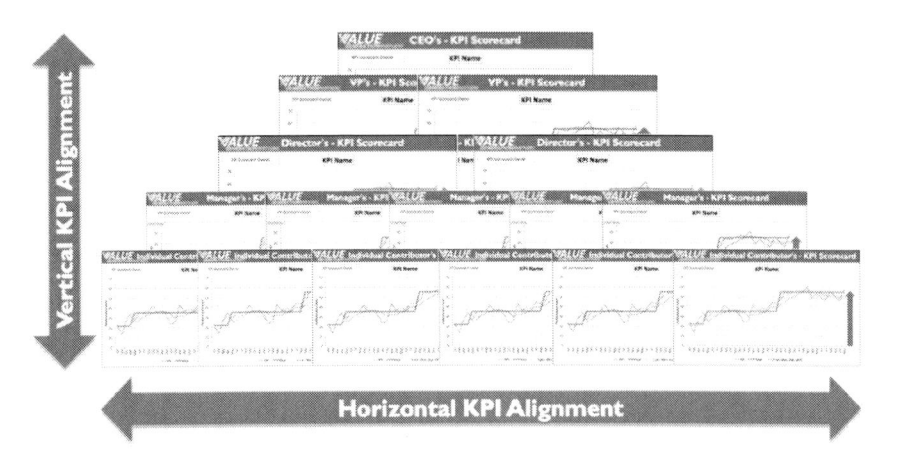

Balancing the scorecards across categories of financial, customer, internal processes, and learning and growth ensures focus is given across the critical areas of the business.

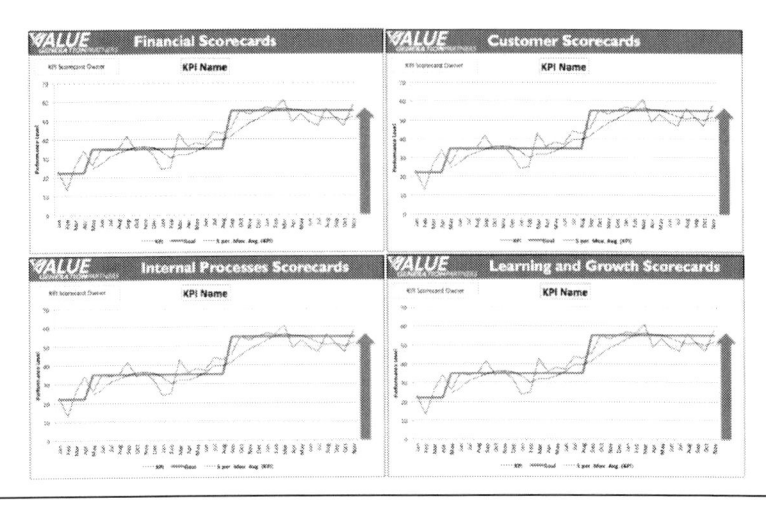

Step Six: Sustain Results with Scorecards

Each scorecard contains specific and common information as described in the following image:

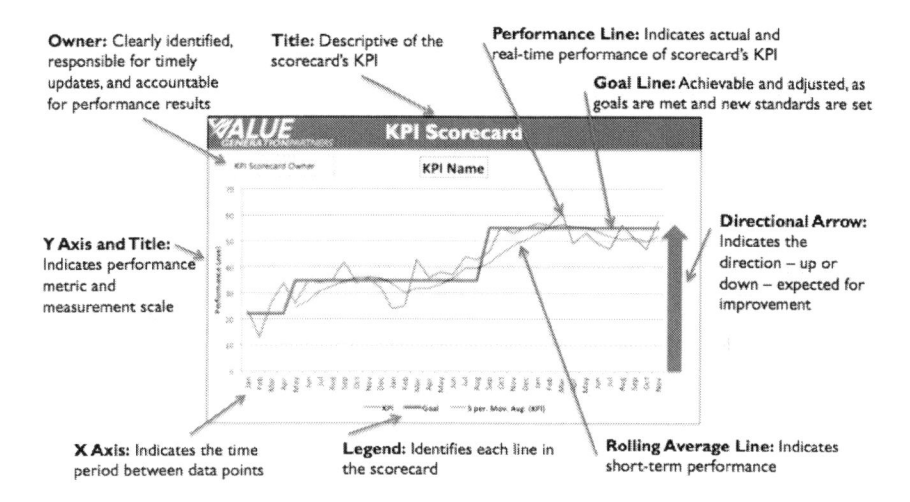

Owner: Clearly identified, responsible for timely updates, and accountable for performance results

Title: Descriptive of the scorecard's KPI

Performance Line: Indicates actual and real-time performance of scorecard's KPI

Goal Line: Achievable and adjusted, as goals are met and new standards are set

Y Axis and Title: Indicates performance metric and measurement scale

Directional Arrow: Indicates the direction – up or down – expected for improvement

X Axis: Indicates the time period between data points

Legend: Identifies each line in the scorecard

Rolling Average Line: Indicates short-term performance

Benefits of balanced and cascading scorecards include:

- Support organizational understanding of strategic goals and objectives
- Support execution of strategic goals and objectives
- Provide indicators of progress toward strategic goals and objectives
- Allow for timely changes and adjustments in approach based on results
- Method to measure individual performance and development opportunities
- Input for one-on-one coaching sessions between managers and employees
- Alignment of the organization toward common strategic goals and objectives

Additional considerations for implementing balanced and cascading scorecards includes determining the number of scorecards necessary for each level and position. While the number of scorecards is dependent on the level of the position and its impact on the strategic goals and objectives, each identified and defined KPI in Step Two: Understand the KPIs will have a scorecard to measure, monitor, and manage the results. Note: The level one leader may have several

Step Six: Sustain Results with Scorecards

scorecards, while a level six individual contributor may have one or two scorecards.

Scorecards are most effective when reviewed in weekly one-on-one sessions. Balanced and cascading scorecards typically measure outputs or results. When the scorecards and KPIs indicate results are not as planned, the approaches defined in Step Five: Execute with Rigor and Discipline are employed. Project Management for Success, Problem Solving for Success, and Workshop Facilitation for Success are efficient and effective approaches to understand and improve inputs that drive business results tracked on scorecards.

Defining and deploying balanced and cascading scorecards starts with a clear understanding of the organization's strategic goals and objectives and associated KPIs. Then, working with the level one leader, define and deploy scorecards for each of the defined KPIs – those that will drive organizational performance necessary to achieve strategic goals and objectives, as defined by the organizational strategy maps. Deploy these top-level scorecards by making them clearly understood and visible to the entire organization.

Now, progressing to direct reports of the top-level position, work with each level two leaders to define and deploy their critical scorecards. During this process, in order to secure ownership and sustainability, it is critical to work directly with those who will own the scorecards (level two leaders) and their leader – level one. And then this is done at each level in the organization. Once each level of scorecards is developed, communicated, and made visible to the entire organization, progress toward strategic success will become visible; improvement efforts and directional changes then may be implemented, where necessary.

Step Seven: Salute the Organization

Step Seven of Strategy Driven for Success is Salute the Organization. Key elements of this step include 1) celebrating the organization's success of achieving strategic goals and objectives and 2) delivering required strategic results, as well as 3) recognition of organizational team members and their contributions toward the initiatives and projects that led to achievement of the strategic goals and objectives.

Vince Lombardi is quoted as saying, "The achievements of an organization are the results of the combined effort of each individual." Stephen Covey said, "The bottom line is, when people are crystal clear about the most important priorities of the organization and team they work with and prioritized their work around those top priorities, not only are they many times more productive, they discover they have the time they need to have a whole life." The strength and success of an organization's achievement of strategic goals and objectives is highly dependent on a strong organizational culture.

Process to Salute the Organization:

1. Conduct celebration and recognition events for successful achievement of strategic goals and objectives that resulted through the execution of initiatives and projects
2. Motivate teams and employees to continue to excel at achieving additional strategic goals and objectives through execution of initiatives and projects

Benefits of saluting the organization include:

- Provide sense of purpose
- Communicate business results
- Reinforce positive outcomes
- Collaborative environment
- Sense of belonging
- Skill development and learning
- Silos and barriers do not exist
- Efficiently and effectively completing and delivering strategic results that individuals alone cannot
- Inclusive environment in which teams work toward common goals

Step Seven: Salute the Organization

All of the Strategy Driven for Success steps are important and necessary, yet organizational recognition and celebration is critical to the successful achievement of strategic goals and objectives and to enhance organizational culture. Recognition and celebration should provide positive reinforcement, in a setting instrumental to personal reward, and should be conducted or attended by leadership and senior management.

Methods and approaches to saluting the organization include:

- Monthly newsletters
- Website or intranet
- Special celebration ceremonies and recognition meetings
- Company gifts (logo hats, shirts, mugs, etc.)
- Gift certificates
- Team, staff, and leadership meetings

Saluting the organization should be carried out in a public forum, providing team members with recognition and motivation from leadership and peers. This step in Strategy Driven for Success ensures that the organization and teams will support the next strategic goal and others will be motivated to join future initiatives and projects necessary to achieve strategic goals and objectives.

Summary: Strategy Driven for Success

Strategy Driven for Success consists of applying processes and tools to define, deploy, execute, and achieve strategic goals and objectives. It may be applied at the corporate, organizational, business unit, functional, or department level. Michael Porter, Harvard professor at The Institute for Strategy and Competitiveness, once said, "The best CEOs I know are teachers, and at the core of what they teach is strategy." All levels of successful leaders and managers apply strategic approach and methodology to ensure their organizations, customers, suppliers, and employees succeed.

SUCCESS
- Set the Strategic Goals
- Understand the KPIs
- Create Cultural Engagement
- Construct the Initiatives
- Execute with Rigor and Discipline
- Sustain Results with Scorecards
- Salute the Organization

This simple and comprehensive seven-step approach, called Strategy Driven for Success, may be applied in any industry or business regardless of size – healthcare, construction, manufacturing, service, hospitality, non-profit, government, financial, etc. This handbook is designed for leaders and managers of all levels to define and deploy strategic goals and objectives. It combines the necessary elements of strategy definition and deployment into the following seven-step Strategy Driven for Success process:

1. **Set the Strategic Goals** – collect voice of... customer, business, employee, process, and competitor; create organizational level SIPOCs; conduct SWOT analysis; draft SMART strategic goals and objectives; conduct force field analysis and refine strategic

Summary: Strategy Drive for Success

    goals and objectives; define, communicate, and cascade strategy maps
2. **Understand the KPIs** – define, align, and cascade key performance indicators (KPIs) through the organization
3. **Create Cultural Engagement** – engage the culture with change leadership, conflict resolution, consensus building, motivating individuals, and team building
4. **Construct the Initiatives** – identify potential initiatives and projects, prioritize potential initiatives and projects, align initiatives and projects with strategic goals and objectives
5. **Execute with Rigor and Discipline** – execute the initiatives and projects to achieve the strategic goals and objectives using Project Management for Success, Problem Solving for Success, and/or Workshop Facilitation for Success
6. **Sustain Results with Scorecards** – define, align, and cascade KPI scorecards through the organization
7. **Salute the Organization** – recognize the organization, teams, and individuals – and celebrate success!

Key to Strategy Driven for Success is timely, concise, and appropriate communication. George Bernard Shaw was quoted as saying, "The single biggest problem in communication is the illusion that it has taken place." As you execute the seven-step strategy driven approach, ensure that in each step careful consideration is given to the impact on the many and various stakeholders and how that impact is communicated.

Benefits of timely and concise communication include:

- Understanding of strategic goals and objectives
- Facilitate support for the strategic goals and objectives
- Clarification on purpose, vision, mission, and core values
- Understanding and clarification on KPIs and scorecards
- Clarification of roles and responsibilities
- Status of the strategic initiatives and projects

Congratulations on achieving strategic goals and objectives by applying Strategy Driven for Success! We wish you continued success in your pursuit of strategic success, thereby generating greater organizational value!

Index

5

5 Why
　Root-Cause Analysis, 61, 64, 71

A

A3, 60, 61, 62, 63, 64, 66
A3 – Problem Solving for Success Worksheet, 61, 62, 63, 64, 65, 66
A3 Thinking
　Lean Thinking, 60, 62
Action Plan, 19, 38, 56, 65, 71, 72
Adjourning, 41
Affinity Diagram, 16, 45, 71
Alderfer's ERG Theory, 34, 35
Analyze, 8, 9, 10, 11, 12, 56

B

Balanced Scorecard, 22, 73, 75
Belonging, 36
Block Diagrams, 12
Brainstorming, 15, 16, 45, 71
Budget, 8, 45, 46, 48, 54, 56, 69

C

C&E
　Cause-and-Effect Diagram, Fishbone Diagram, Ishikawa Diagram, 71
Cascading Scorecards, 20, 24, 73, 74, 75, 76
Cause-and-Effect Matrix
　X-Y Matrix, 71
Celebrate, i, iii, 2, 29, 41, 43, 55, 56, 59, 61, 69, 80
Change Control Plan, 55, 58
Change Leaders, 26, 27
Change Leadership, 26, 28
Change Resistors, 28
Charter, 53, 69, 70, 71, 72
checklist, 17, 55, 56, 57, 58, 59
Cognitive Evaluation Theory (CET) of Motivation, 34
Concise, 2, 38, 40, 67, 80
Contact List, 55, 57, 58
Continuous Improvement, 6
CTC
　Critical-to-Customer, 5, 12, 13
Cultural Engagement, 1, 23, 25, 80
Cultural Engagement for Success, 25

D

Define, 3, 4, 5, 12, 16, 17, 19, 20, 22, 23, 31, 32, 47, 49, 65, 66, 71
Desired, 14, 26, 66
DMAIC, 60

E

Esteem, 36
Existence, 35
Expected, 4, 12, 13, 39, 50, 72
Extrinsic Motivators, 34

F

Facilitation, 15, 19, 25, 33, 69
Flow-down, 47
FMEA
　Failure Modes and Effects Analysis, 71
Force Field Analysis, 18, 19
Forming, 39

G

Growth, 21, 24, 35, 74

Index

H
Herzberg's Two-Factor Theory, 34, 35
Hoshin Kanri, 20
Hygiene factors, 35

I
Intrinsic Motivators, 34
Issue Management Plan, 55, 58

K
KPI
  Key Performance Indicator, 2, 7, 8, 9, 10, 23, 24, 73, 75, 80

L
Lean Six Sigma
  LSS, 60
Lessons-Learned, 56
Lessons-Learned Plan, 55, 56, 59
Lifecycle, 56

M
Maslow's Hierarchy of Needs, 34, 35, 36
McClelland's Acquired Needs Theory, 34, 37
Measure, 24
Mind Mapping, 16, 71
Minutes, 55, 58, 59
Mission, 2, 3, 4, 21, 26, 28, 38, 42, 80
Mitigate, 15, 19
Monitor, 27, 29, 37, 66
Motivating Individuals, 1, 37, 38, 80
Motivators, 35

N
Nominal, 33
Norming, 40

O
Operational Excellence, 14

P
Pairwise Comparison, 33
PDCA
  PDSA, 60, 62
Performing, 41
Peter Drucker, 17, 23, 26
Physiological, 36
Policy Deployment, 20
Problem, 61, 62, 63, 64, 65, 66, 67
Problem Solving, 61, 62, 63, 64, 65, 66, 67
Problem Solving for Success, 2, 17, 53, 61, 62, 63, 64, 65, 66, 67, 72, 76, 80
Problems, 60
Process, 1, 5, 6, 8, 9, 10, 11, 12, 13, 15, 16, 21, 22, 27, 30, 32, 33, 39, 41, 45, 46, 47, 55, 56, 60, 61, 62, 63, 64, 66, 67, 68, 71, 72, 76, 79
Procurement, 55, 56, 58
Project Lifecycle, 56
Project Management for Success, 2, 53, 54, 55, 56, 57, 58, 59, 60, 76, 80
Project-Close, 56
Pugh
  Concept Selection, 71
Pugh Matrix, 71
Purpose, 2, 3, 4, 21, 28, 38, 39, 42, 70, 77, 80

Q
Quality Management, 55, 58

R
RACI, 55, 58, 71
Rapid Problem Solving for Success, 62

Index

Relatedness, 35
Report, 62, 77
Requirements, 5, 55, 57, 59
Resource Plan, 55, 58, 59
Risk Management Plan, 55, 58
Root Cause, 61, 63, 66

S

Safety, 36
Salute, 2, 25, 53, 54, 55, 60, 61, 67, 72, 73, 77, 80
Schedule, 38, 54, 55, 56, 58, 59, 65, 66, 69
Scope, 38, 54, 56, 57, 70
Scorecards, 2, 6, 20, 22, 24, 73, 74, 75, 76, 80
Self-Actualization, 36
Shainin, 60
SIPOC, 5, 8, 9, 10, 11, 12, 13, 15, 45, 71
Six Sigma, 60
SMART, 1, 5, 8, 9, 10, 11, 12, 16, 17, 47, 61, 63, 69, 79
SME
 Subject Matter Expert, 12, 19, 70
Solution, 2, 53, 61, 64, 65, 66, 80
Solution Implementation, 65
Solutions, 64, 65, 66
Solution-Selection Matrix, 71
Step Five
 Execute Solutions, 53, 65
 Execute the Cultural Engagement Plan, 25
 Execute the Plan, 53, 59
 Execute the Workshop, 54, 68, 70
 Execute with Rigor and Discipline, 45, 53, 76
Step Four
 Clarify Roles and Responsibilities, 54, 68, 70
 Construct Solutions, 53, 64
 Construct the Initiatives, 25, 45
 Construct the Plan, 53, 58

Step One
 Set the Cultural Engagement Strategy, 25
 Set the Strategic Goals, 5
 Set-up the Project, 53, 57
 Set-up the Workshop Charter, 53, 68, 69
 State Problem and Goal, 53, 62, 63
Step Seven
 Salute Cultural Engagement, 25
 Salute the Organization, 73, 77
 Salute the Team, 53, 54, 60, 67, 69, 72
Step Six
 Share Status of Workshop, 54, 68, 71
 Share the Cultural Engagement Status, 25
 Sign-off and Close the Project, 53, 59
 Sustain Results with Scorecards, 24, 54, 73
 Sustain Solutions, 53, 65, 66
Step Three
 Communicate the Desired Culture, 25
 Conduct Root Cause Analysis, 53, 63
 Create Cultural Engagement, 23, 25
 Create the Team, 53, 54, 57, 58, 68, 70
Step Two
 Understand Current Condition, 53, 63
 Understand the Current Culture, 25
 Understand the KPIs, 5, 23, 69, 70, 73, 75
 Understand the Logistics, 54, 68, 69
 Understand the Requirements, 53, 57
Storming, 40

Index

Strategic Goals, 1, 2, 3, 4, 5, 6, 7, 8, 9, 10, 11, 12, 14, 15, 16, 17, 18, 19, 20, 21, 22, 23, 24, 25, 26, 27, 28, 29, 30, 32, 34, 38, 45, 46, 47, 48, 49, 50, 51, 53, 54, 55, 60, 67, 68, 69, 70, 71, 72, 73, 74, 75, 76, 77, 78, 79, 80
Strategy Deployment, 20
Strategy Driven for Success, i, iii, vii, 1, 2, 5, 17, 20, 23, 25, 45, 53, 73, 77, 78, 79, 80
Strategy Maps, 1, 3, 4, 5, 14, 16, 17, 20, 21, 22, 24, 45, 46, 47, 76, 80
Sustain, 2, 24, 53, 54, 61, 66, 73, 80
SWOT, 1, 5, 6, 8, 9, 10, 11, 12, 13, 14, 15, 16, 71, 79

T

Toolbox, 55, 56, 57, 59
Training Plan, 71
Transformation, 6

V

Value Stream, 15, 16, 45, 47
Values, 2, 3, 4, 21, 22, 26, 31, 80
Virtual, 39
Vision, 2, 3, 4, 21, 26, 27, 28, 38, 39, 73, 76, 80
Voice of Business, 6, 8
Voice of Competitor, 6, 11, 12
Voice of Customer, 6, 7
Voice of Employee, 6, 9
Voice of Process, 6, 10, 11
Voice of…, 6

W

Wait-and-Seers, 27
Workshop Facilitation for Success, 2, 53, 67, 68, 69, 70, 71, 72, 76, 80

X

X-Matrix, 20

Printed in Great Britain
by Amazon